COMBAT
CARRIERS

COMBAT CARRIERS

Flying Action on Carriers at Sea

Tony Holmes

Motorbooks International
Publishers & Wholesalers ®

Dedication

This book is dedicated to A W 'Bill' Bedford OBE AFC RAeS, who sadly passed away during its compilation.

This edition first published in 1998 by Motorbooks International, Publishers & Wholesalers, 729 Prospect Avenue, PO Box 1, Osceola, WI 54020, USA.

© Tony Holmes 1998

Previously published by Airlife Publishing Ltd, Shrewsbury, England.

Library of Congress Cataloging-in-Publication Data is available

ISBN 0-7603–0572-2

Printed in Hong Kong

Contents

Acknowledgements

I have always been made to feel most welcome by the various crews of the carriers on which I have embarked over the years, and although I cannot personally name all of those individuals who have helped me during the compilation of this book due to the restriction on space, the following men and women have all proved invaluable in seeing the project through to fruition.

Royal Navy/Royal Fleet Auxiliary/Fleet Air Arm

Lt-Cdr Peter West, FONAC PRO; First Officer Tony Sherlock, RFA PRO; Cdr Chris Thomas, HMS *Ark Royal*; Rod Fredericksen, British Aerospace; Lt-Cdr Dave Baddams, Lt-Cdr Dick Hawkins and Lt Dicky Payne, No 800 Sqn; POs Chris North and Bryan Sharkey.

Fleet PR and DPR Navy

Lorraine Coulton and Keith Hanman.

US Navy

Lt(jg) Charlie Brown, PAO Naval Air Forces Pacific; Cdr Bob Anderson, Chief of Public Information USCINCEUR; Lt-Cdr Dave Wells and Lt Brett Kelly, PAOs on CV 64 in 1995; Lts Jeff Breslau and Meg Arthur, PAOs on CV 64 in 1996; Cdr Dave Philman, CO of VFA-151; Lt Hal Schmitt, VFA-137; Lts Curt Seth and John Solma, VF-2; the photographic section aboard CV 64; the crew of 'Hunter 613', Lts John-Paul Ayubi and Mike Collins, AW2 Justin Tate and AW3 Matt McElroy; Cdr Jim Winter, Seventh Fleet Representative, Western Australia; Lt-Cdr Tom Twomey.

Civilians

Michael O'Leary; Eve Taylor; Robin Surrich, US Consulate, Western Australia; Vic Jeffrey, Fleet PRO, RAN; Gary Sheehan and Richard Siudak, ANA; Tim Vickeridge; Peter Mersky; Mick Firth, Preston Helicopters; Julian Holdaway, Stephenson Aviation Ltd; Dave Wilton, BAR; Rod Burden; Ian Glanville, British Airways.

Introduction

As early as July 1921, wartime US Army Air Service hero Brig-Gen William 'Billy' Mitchell had proved that even the most heavily armoured vessel was vulnerable to attack from the skies by sinking the former German battleship *Ostfriesland* with bombs dropped from a fleet of Martin MB-2s. Watching this graphic demonstration, staged off the coast of Virginia, was an assembled throng of ranking soldiers and sailors from the US armed forces, plus assorted military attachés and politicians from Washington DC. Although many were sceptical as to the value of such bombing trials, and instigator Mitchell was eventually court martialled for 'making statements contrary to military order and discipline' as a result of the resistance he encountered in the wake of his demonstration, from that moment on the once mighty battleship was no longer the undisputed 'King of the Waves'.

Over seven decades later the combat carriers of the 1990s are capable of far greater destruction than could have ever been imagined at the turn of the century. Indeed, a single aircraft equipped with the relevant conventional ordnance and launched from the deck of a 'super carrier' could all but sink the most heavily-armed, and armoured, battleship of World War Two.

Although the balance of power on the high seas has irrevocably shifted from the battleship to the aircraft carrier, one factor has remained constant between the two weapons of war – the human element. Many thousands of men were required to crew the 'steel monsters' of decades ago, and a similar situation still exists today – a *Nimitz*-class carrier with an air wing embarked regularly deploys with over 5,000 sailors aboard.

In this volume I have attempted to imbue the reader with a feeling of what daily life is like for the men (and women) who work 'up on the roof' of a modern carrier within the US and Royal Navys. In so doing, I have limited my coverage of what occurs 'below decks', and therefore must apologise to those souls who rarely get to breathe the sea air, mixed with hydraulic fluid and JP-4 – this volume is most definitely one for the 'brown shoes'!

Witnessing the daily ritual of flight ops out at sea is a truly awesome experience. It provides an 'in your face' assault on all five senses from the moment you step out onto the steel deck. Your field of vision is filled with the sight of aircraft launching at break-neck speeds over the shortest possible distance, and then returning later to literally 'crash' back aboard in the most abrupt, but nevertheless controlled, fashion. The ear-splitting din of jet engines screeching on full military power, or phase five afterburner, provides the soundtrack for this 'theatre at sea', which is occasionally punctuated by the God-like voice of the Air Boss, or Commander (AIR), barking out instructions over the ship's PA system.

Accompanying the sights and sounds of 'blue water ops' is the smell of carrier aviation – a heady mix of hydraulic fluid, JP-4, burnt rubber, scorched metal and the sea. Similarly, the taste of the deck that coats your face and stings the back of your throat as the ship steams at 30 knots into the wind is heavily flavoured with fuel and salt spray. It is only properly eradicated at the end of the day by another taste synonymous with US carriers – the cheeseburger, accompanied by a copious quantity of fries!

Finally, deck ops touch you in a way that no other form of military aviation can. The heat exhausted by a Hornet, Sea Harrier or Tomcat as it taxies just feet away envelopes you in an invisible blanket so warm that it induces an instant sweat. When the same jet is throttled up for launch, the sonic shock waves emitted from the engines as they feed off their high octane mix of fuel and air pass straight through flesh and bone with little resistance. The rasping gale spilling over the bow and thundering down the deck also touches you from head to foot as you fight to stay balanced on a pitching steel 'roof', some 90 ft above the sea.

This seemingly alien environment is the exclusive domain of the young and the fit – both in body and mind. All five senses have to be effectively interacting with each other in order to ensure one's survival up on deck. There is no room for complacency, nor any margin for error.

Over the past decade I have been fortunate enough to observe carrier operations from the best possible vantage point – out on the steel deck, surrounded by the organised chaos that is naval aviation in action. In the ten years since my first volume on US Navy carriers was published, much has changed in respect to the perceived 'enemy', resulting global threats and the force deemed necessary to cope with such aggressors. Proven combat aircraft types like the Corsair II, Intruder and Sea King have 'passed the torch' onto newer designs, whilst veteran jets like the Tomcat and Sea Harrier have had their capabilities upgraded so as to allow them to fight on in differing roles well into the 21st century. A number of famous ships and squadrons have also been decommissioned and disestablished, and the aircraft they operated either placed in storage or simply scrapped – the US Navy has lost a third of its 'blue water' units and decommissioned six frontline 'super carriers' in the past decade, receiving just four *Nimitz*-class CVNs in their place.

Despite shrinking defence budgets, and associated cuts in equipment and manpower levels, aircraft carriers will remain the chosen instrument of power projection for those few countries that can afford to operate them for the foreseeable future. Who knows what will be launching off the decks of 'super carriers' when I sit down to write the introduction to my third volume on naval aviation in 2007?!

Tony Holmes
Sevenoaks, Kent

WestPac 95

Date: April 1995
Location: Indian Ocean
Aircraft Carrier: USS *Constellation* (CV 64)

T he ultimate test of effectiveness for an aircraft carrier is an extended deployment in foreign waters, thousands of miles from home. For the US Navy, this challenge takes the form of a *WestPac*. Usually comprising a single 'super carrier' supported by numerous escort vessels and supply ships, the *WestPac* lasts six months and sees the battle group sail as far afield as the Persian Gulf.

For many years the 'only game in town' when it came to fighter protection of both the air wing and the battle group, Northrop Grumman's once mighty Tomcat is now in the twilight of its lengthy career. Ironically enough, it is only in the past five years that the aircraft has at last attained maturity with respect to its powerplant following the introduction of the F-14D. This 'coming of age' has seen the fighter develop into a true multi-role machine with the addition of mission avionics that have allowed the jet to take on the precision bombing role. Vastly superior to the F-14A both in terms of its General Electric F110-GE-400 turbofan engines and state-of-the-art AN/APG-71

radar, linked with a digital avionics suite based on MIL-STD-1553G multiprocessors, only fifty-five (thirty-seven new-build and eighteen upgraded F-14A airframes) D-model Tomcats have been made available to the Navy. These were originally supplied to three frontline units and one training squadron, although with the recent transition of VF-11 'Red Rippers' to F-14Bs, just VF-31 'Tomcatters' and VF-2 'Bounty Hunters' are left operating the 'Super Tomcat' at sea. One of fourteen D-models embarked on board CV 64 for *WestPac 95*, BuNo 163895 was the tenth new-build 'Super Tomcat' constructed by Grumman at Bethpage, and was delivered to the Navy on 31 October 1990.

Below:
Wearing his distinctive yellow 'float-coat' and similarly coloured polo neck shirt, the flightdeck chief uses hand signals to converse with the crew of 'Bullet 111' (BuNo 159613) while a 'white-shirted' safety crewman inspects the nose gear's hydraulic retraction jack prior to clearing it for launch. The F-14D's distinctive General Electric/Martin-Marietta dual undernose sensor pod, housing a GE Aerospace Electronic Systems AN/AAS Infra-Red Scanner/Tracker (IRST – domed on the right) and Northrop AN/AAX-1 Television Camera Set (TCS – flat on the left), can be clearly seen in this view; a red anti-collision light is scabbed on to the bottom of the protuberance. This particular jet was originally delivered to the fleet as an A-model as long ago as September 1975, but was given a new lease of life when rebuilt as one of eighteen F-14D(R)s in 1991 at Grumman's Bethpage works. It was reissued to VF-11 as 'Ripper 106' in 1992, and completed a *WestPac* with the unit on board USS *Carl Vinson* (CVN 70) as part of CVW-14 in 1994 before being reassigned to VF-2.

For the US Navy's Third and Seventh Fleets, the vast expanses of the Pacific and, more recently, Indian Oceans have for decades been their 'beat'. The force's proud combat history was created in the warm waters of the western Pacific during World War Two, and today these same locations see the latest generation of naval aviators building on the proud traditions of fifty-plus years ago. Since that time, the coastal seas off Korea and Vietnam have also lapped at the hulls of carrier task forces in action, while in the past two decades US Navy carriers have ventured further westward into the Indian Ocean, where they have supported thousands of sorties over the Persian Gulf. One of the veterans of *WestPac* deployments over the past thirty years is the battle-seasoned carrier USS *Constellation* (CV 64), which has completed no fewer than seventeen since entering Navy service in 1961. In that time it has seen both war and peace, examples of the former including the record eight combat cruises the vessel undertook during the Vietnam conflict. Indeed, the carrier was on a *WestPac* in August 1964 when two Seventh Fleet destroyers were attacked by North Vietnamese patrol boats while cruising near to the communist coastline. 'Connie's' air wing, along with aircraft from the smaller USS *Ticonderoga* (CVA 14), duly flew the first air strikes – codenamed *Pierce Arrow* – against North Vietnam on 5

Well in the groove and looking good for an 'OK Three' pass landing, the pilot of 'Bullet 105' (BuNo 164603 – the second to last Tomcat ever built) rides the centred 'meatball' of the LLD (Landing Light Device) down onto the steel deck. The fighter will be doing about 140 knots at this point in its recovery, and should the pilot suffer a 'bolter' – the hook fails to engage any of the four arrestor wires, or hits the deck and 'bolts' over them – upon 'hitting' onto the deck, he has an abundance of thrust available (27,600lb from each engine to be precise) to allow him to regain height and go around again.

August. In more peaceful times, CV 64 debuted the F/A-18 Hornet in frontline US Navy service when it undertook *WestPac 85* with VFA's -25 and -113 embarked.

A decade later, and with a $800-million/three-year Service Life Extension Program (SLEP) behind it, CV 64 once again found itself on *WestPac* for the first time since 1989. When the carrier slipped its moorings at its NAS North Island home within the vast port of San Diego in early November 1994, this marked the start of a deployment which both the ship's crew of over 4,000 men and the embarked air wing of near on 1,500 personnel had been working towards since the vessel returned to California from the Philadelphia Naval Shipyard in July 1993.

At various bases up and down the west coast, squadrons within CVW-2 had been completing an eighteen-month-long cycle of

Basking in the warmth of a typically sunny autumn day in the port city of Fremantle, Western Australia, VF-2's 'CAG bird' (BuNo 161163) takes pride of place beneath 'Connie's' impressive island structure. Since the advent of the Tactical Paint Scheme in the early 1980s, only the designated CAG aircraft and the squadron commander's jet have

been allowed to wear full-colour markings, and even these have varied in size and tone depending on the CO's attitude to unit heraldry. Fortunately for marking aficionados, VF-2's boss at the time, Cdr L Scott 'Scooter' Lamoreaux, respected the proud history of the unit and avidly encouraged the decoration of 'Bullets 100'

and '101' in full squadron regalia. One of six F-14D(R)s assigned to the 'Bounty Hunters' in 1995, this jet was the 390th Tomcat built for the Navy and had originally been delivered from Bethpage as an F-14A in February 1981.

training operations in preparation for the ultimate challenge – *WestPac 95*. Within hours of the carrier sailing into the Pacific, she had recovered on board some seventy-five combat aircraft ranging in size from the F-14D Tomcat to the SH-60F Seahawk. The inherent capability of this powerful force would duly bestow upon the battle group the respect it deserved from potential aggressors, and thus allow it to operate independently of land-based support. In addition to its air wing, 'Connie' was joined by the *Spruance*-class destroyer *Kinkaid* (DD 965), the *Los Angeles*-class attack submarine *Topeka* (SSN 754) and the *Kilauea*-class ammunition ship *Kiska* (AE 35); once in Hawaiian waters, the final elements of her battle group (*Ticonderoga*-class missile cruisers *Chosin* (CG 65) and *Lake Erie* (CG 70) and the oiler *Cimarron* (AO 177) – name ship of this class) rendezvoused with the carrier to finalise the complement of Cruiser-Destroyer Group 1.

The first test for CVW-2, led by CAG Capt. David C Nichols, came in late November when the air wing participated in Operation *Beachcrest 95*, off the Japanese island of Okinawa. During the ten-day exercise, naval aircraft operated both alongside and against USAF F-15Cs and USMC F/A-18s, based at Kadena AFB, in a series of combat air support (CAS), defensive air combat (DACT) and offensive and defensive counter-air (OCA/DCA) missions. One unit that found the CAS sorties particularly relevant was the F/A-18C-equipped VMFA-323 'Death Rattlers', who had the distinction of being the only USMC unit within CVW-2 – 231 members of the squadron were embarked on the 'Connie' for the entire cruise. Many of their missions were flown in support of their 'mud Marine'

The average landing run for a fast jet recovering back on board is roughly 320ft, and the resistance of the arrestor gear is preset for the varying weights of the aircraft that comprise a modern air wing. For example, an F/A-18C in typical peacetime configuration will weigh in at roughly 42,000lb when it crosses the carrier ramp, while a TARPS-equipped F-14D can easily tip the scales at over 71,000lb when it engages the 'cross-deck pendant' ('wire'). Therefore, the stopping power generated by the arrestor cable engines buried immediately below the flightdeck has to be increased to pull the heavier jet up in the same distance as the lighter aircraft. The 'wire' has a service life of just 100 landings.

brethren 'invading' the numerous ranges in the Okinawan exercise area.

More low-key exercises off South Korea then followed, which included low-level navigation flights, aerial tours of the Demilitarised Zone, and air-to-ground ordnance delivery missions for the Hornets, before the battle group headed westward to Hong Kong and then Singapore for Christmas and New Year respectively. With the festive season over, 'Connie' started a new line period as she headed west out of the Pacific and charted a course for the Persian Gulf. Once in the Middle East, the air wing commenced its ceaseless cycle of patrols into what pilots refer to as 'The Box' – the No Fly Zone imposed over southern Iraq by the UN in the aftermath of the 1991 war. These flights are an integral part of Operation *Southern Watch*, and US Navy aircraft have performed their fair share of sorties over the area in the past six years, occasionally having to resort to force when fired upon by belligerent Iraqi SAM and AAA batteries.

Prior to the carrier arriving on station, the *WestPac* 'freshmen' of VFA-137 'Kestrels' had forward deployed nine F/A-18Cs, supported by two EA-6Bs, to Sheikh Isa air base, on the island state of Bahrain, as an advanced party to smooth the way for the rest of CVW-2 – they had flown a sortie over Iraq en route. Once in the Gulf itself, the air wing completed a straight seventy-three-day stretch 'on the line' alongside aircraft from the USAF, Royal Saudi Air Force, RAF and French Air Force. The F-14Ds of VF-2 'Bounty Hunters' were kept particularly busy flying both DCA and TARPS recce missions deep in

The bow of the carrier is traditionally the home of the light strike community when on board ship and, as this shot shows, CVW-2 did not break with tradition when embarked on CV 64. Two Lot XV F/A-18Cs of VMFA-323 ('Snake 200'/BuNo 164721) and VFA-137 ('Falcon 406'/BuNo 164715) are seen being turned around between sorties off the coast of southern Western Australia, both jets being fitted with Mk 7 Cluster Bomb Unit (CBU) dispensers on their respective outer wing pylons. Having participated in the successful up-loading of the CBU onto the pylon of the Marine Hornet, the red-shirted armourer, or 'B-B stacker', is seen in the process of removing the electricity lead from the jet's ground power socket.

The deck of the ship can become a little 'gridlocked' during the minutes preceding the next cycle of launches, with as many as twenty aircraft having to sit patiently in line behind the four catapults as the carrier turns into wind and accelerates up to thirty knots to enable flying operations to commence. Queuing up behind bow cat two, the pilot of 'Snake 202' (BuNo 164724) keeps a watchful eye on the armourer as the latter checks the mounting lug on the port AIM-9L. MCAS Miramar-based VMFA-323 'Diamondbacks' is presently one of just three fleet-qualified USMC units regularly participating in 'blue water' ops with the US Navy – VMFAs -251 and -312 are the other two squadrons, both of which are based at MCAS Beaufort in South Carolina.

All the jets within CVW-2 were exhibiting serious signs of wear by April 1995, having been on cruise since early November 1994. A typical example was 'Switch 302' (BuNo 164897) of VFA-151, flown by squadron XO, Cdr Dave 'Deke' Philman, who was in the process of completing his fourth *WestPac* – he had previously deployed in A-7Es, his last cruise in the Corsair II being with VA-27 in 1990 when the 'SLUF' participated in its final *WestPac*. Philman later assumed command of the 'Vigilantes' in February 1996 and led the unit on its *WestPac 97*.

'Switch 301' (BuNo 164896) feels the heat as it sits behind the cat two JBD (Jet Blast Deflector) just moments away from launch – note both the TER (Triple Ejector Rack), fitted with 25lb Mk 76 'blue bombs', on the port outer pylon and the Loral (Ford Aerospace) AN/AAS-38 FLIR (Forward-Looking Infra-Red) targeting pod sited just above the port undercarriage leg. VFA-151 received all twelve of its Lot XV F/A-18Cs directly from the McDonnell Douglas plant at St Louis in early 1993, thus allowing the unit's maintenance department to be totally familiar with each jet's technical history. This has greatly improved the serviceability rate within the squadron, and has allowed engineers to evenly schedule the jets into the flying programme in order to keep airframe hours constant fleet-wide.

'The Box', as well as performing their routine CAP duties for the battle group.

With dedicated electronic warfare assets being rather 'thin on the ground' in the Middle East, the four EA-6Bs of VAQ-131 'Lancers' were in constant demand to support UN aircraft flying into the potentially hazardous airspace over southern Iraq. As an indication of the constant cycle of ops undertaken by the unit, 730 hours of flying were completed in the 175-plus sorties the Prowlers flew in the first three months of 1995.

With the Lot XV F/A-18Cs being the most numerous type within CVW-2 (thirty-six jets split between three units, none of which had been on a cruise since 1991), it came as no surprise to find that the light strike community performed the lion's share of the patrol tasking assigned to 'Connie'. The busiest Hornet operator of them all was VMFA-323, which completed no fewer than 411 sorties during the enforcement of the No Fly Zone; this mission total boiled down to 820.4 hours spent on station over, or off the coast of, southern Iraq. When not on station, CVW-2 participated in a number of exotically named exercises with local air forces, including *Beacon Flash* with Royal Omani Air Force Jaguar OSs, Hunter FGA 73s and Hawk 200s, *Eager Archer* with the KAF-18Cs of the Kuwaiti Air Force, and *Nautical Artist* and *Neon Arrow* with F-15S/Cs and Tornado ADVs of the Royal Saudi Air Force. VFA-151 'Vigilante's' sortie total of sixty-plus for all these exercises combined was typical of the number flown by most squadrons within CVW-2 – it had earlier completed 400-plus flights during the *Southern Watch* phase of the cruise.

'Connie' finally 'chopped out' of Operation *Southern Watch* on 21

Above:
VFA-137's CAG aircraft (BuNo 164712) is something of a 'celebrity' machine, being the 10,000th military jet built by McDonnell Douglas at its St Louis, Missouri, plant – the first was a McDonnell FH-1 Phantom navy fighter, which performed its maiden flight in January 1945. Jumping ahead almost fifty years, 'Falcon 400' was delivered to VFA-137 at its NAS Lemoore home on 10 February 1993, being one of twelve Lot XV jets issued to the unit as replacements for their weary Lot VIII F/A-18As just prior to the 'Kestrels' joining the revamped CVW-2. With such a pedigree, this machine was always destined to be the 'flagship' of the squadron, and it duly received full-colour tail markings comprising a stylised bird of prey on the outer fin surfaces and a yellow CVW-2 badge inboard – the latter was unique to VFA-137's CAG aircraft. This was further complemented by 'MacAir's' celebratory 10,000th jet nose art, which had sadly been removed by the time the author saw the aircraft once again in October 1996 (see chapter three).

Below:
Like 'Switch 301', this jet (BuNo 164719) is also stored up with Mk 76 training bombs and a FLIR, plus AIM-7F and AIM-9L rounds. The aircraft's launch strop has already been slotted into the front of the catapult shuttle and locked into place, while the hydraulic hold-back device to the rear of the nose gear leg has also been connected up. Once instructed that he is correctly attached to the catapult, the pilot will quickly check that his control surfaces are unrestricted and that the jet's mechanicals are functioning as normal. Whilst all this is going on, the squadron's launch safety crewman will also be checking the aircraft externally, and once both parties are happy that things appear to be fit to go, the pilot opens the throttle and the nose gear contracts under the strain of 32,000lb of take-off thrust.

March 1995, and it was doubly fitting that the final patrol should be concluded by a pair of VF-2 F-14Ds, one of which was flown by CAG, Capt. 'Nickel' Nichols. The 'Bounty Hunters' had flown close to 800 sorties, and totalled some 2,050 hours, enforcing the UN Security Council's resolution, making it the high time unit in CVW-2 – the unit's fourteen jets had clocked up 721 hours in just fifteen days during operations in February. Having exited the Straits of Hormuz on 23 March, the carrier plotted a course for the US Navy's favourite liberty port – Perth, Western Australia. Just prior to the battle group pulling into Fremantle Harbour on 8 April, elements of the air wing conducted a limited war-at-sea exercise with the RAN frigate HMAS *Darwin* (F 04), as well as expending several tons of ordnance on the extensive Lancelin weapons range north of Perth. After spending five days alongside, the vessel sailed eastward through the Great Australian Bight to Sydney for another forty-eight-hour port call.

With the *WestPac* now almost over, Cruiser-Destroyer Group 1 split up with the carrier's arrival in Pearl Harbor. Prior to heading east for the final five-day sprint back to San Diego, CV 64 welcomed on board family members from CVW-2 for the traditional 'Tiger Cruise' to California. These lucky individuals got to witness naval aviation in operation at first-hand, culminating in the air wing fly-off on 9 May 1995. It was left to VF-2 to announce 'Connie's' imminent return to San Diego following the successful completion of its first *WestPac* in six years when all fourteen of the unit's Tomcats performed a slick formation fly-by firstly over the city centre, and then their NAS Miramar home. Repeat performances by the remaining units within CVW-2 were played out at several other air stations that same day.

With *Constellation* back in harbour and her air wing dispersed, heavy maintenance was started by both the ship's company and CVW-2 squadron maintainers in preparation for the first work-ups for their next *WestPac*, scheduled for spring 1997.

'Falcon 413' (BuNo 164739) is set upon by squadron armourers in preparation for the reloading of the jet's 570-round ammunition drum, fitted immediately behind the cranked access panel. The belt-mounted 20mm shells can be fed straight into the magazine by a two- to three-man team from the wheeled trolley sat on the deck. The gun team will return to the jet once it has landed back on board and wind the spent belt feeder into an empty ammunition drum, before sending it down to the armoury for reloading.

Embarked Aircraft

VF-2 'Bounty Hunters' – F-14D Tomcat

161163/100	159630/101	164602/102	164350/103
163895/104	164603/105	163897/106	163903/107
163898/110	159613/111	159619/112	159628/114
159600/115	164349/116		

VMFA-323 'Death Rattlers' – F/A-18C Hornet

164721/200	164722/201	164724/202	164725/203
164727/204	164728/205	164730/206	164731/207
164732/210	164733/211	164734/212	164696/214

VFA-151 'Vigilantes' – F/A-18C Hornet

164703/300	164896/301	164897/302	164700/303
164708/304	164710/305	164713/306	164716/307
164719/310	164737/311	164740/312	164865/313

VFA-137 'Kestrels' – F/A-18C Hornet

164712/400	164698/401	164701/402	164704/403
164709/404	164693/405	164715/406	164718/407
164720/410	164707/411	164736/412	164739/413

VAW-116 'Sun Kings' – E-2C Group II Hawkeye

164112/600	164484/601	164487/602	164492/603

HS-2 'Golden Falcons' – SH-60F/HH-60H Seahawk

SH-60F

164079/610	164456/611	164458/612	164088/613

HH-60H

163792/614	163793/615

VAQ-131 'Lancers' – EA-6B Prowler

163398/620	163404/621	163524/622	163525/623

VS-38 'Red Griffins' – S-3B Viking

160573/700	160596/701	160583/702	160126/703
160567/704	160576/705	158872/706	160578/707

VQ-5 'Sea Shadows' 'Det Alpha' – ES-3A Viking

158862/722	159397/726

VRC-30 'Providers' – C-2A*

162173/20	162146/36

* not technically part of CVW-2

One of the highlights of the pre-R&R exercising off Fremantle during *WestPac 95* was a long-range war-at-sea training strike flown by EA-6Bs of VAQ-131 against the Australian frigate HMAS *Darwin* (F 04) – CAG aircraft 'Skybolt 620' (BuNo 163398) was a participant in this exercise. One of thirty-six new-build ICAP II/Block 86 jets delivered to the Navy in the late 1980s, this particular machine saw action in Operation *Desert Storm* with VAQ-130 'Zappers' (again as the unit's 'CAG bird') as part of CVW-3 aboard USS *John F Kennedy* (CV 67). Like the remaining three EA-6Bs deployed on *WestPac 95*, it had been upgraded to Block 89 specification since its escapades in the Gulf.

'Skybolt 620' returns to CV 64 having successfully engaged the *Darwin* on the edge of the battle group's outer defensive perimeter. Emphasising the short duration of its mission (plus the close proximity of the runway at RAAF base Pearce), the aircraft is fitted with just a single external tank rather than the near mandatory pair of fuel cells bolted on for routine 'blue water' ops away from friendly diversionary fields. Three of the remaining four pylons are occupied by ALQ-99F ECM high and low band jamming pods (they also contain a tracking receiver and a built-in exciter/processor for stimulating and categorising electronic signals), which is a standard fit for the Prowler. The 'RATs' (Ram Air Turbines) which generate power to operate the pods can be seen windmilling in the slipstream on the wing-mounted stores.

A 'green-shirted' hook runner visually monitors the retraction of the tailhook back into its position flush with the rear fuselage of the recently returned Prowler. The former signals to the deck edge arrestor gear operator that the aircraft is safe for 'reeling back' by the 'wire' in order to disengage it from the cable.

Right:
The EA-6B is a highly valued asset within any air wing, performing the vital electronic warfare (EW) role in support of the embarked fighter-bomber units. Unlike the latter, which usually deploy up to fifty aircraft to fulfil the strike role, the sole EW squadron on board ship comprises just four Prowlers during a typical cruise. This paucity in numbers means that the workload placed on these jets is appreciably greater than that endured by any other type within the modern CVW – a problem which is compounded by the A-6-generation airframe and systems technology built into the Prowler's structure. By the final month of a *WestPac*, the level of maintenance devoted to keeping the quartet of EA-6Bs aloft is clearly visible in the jets' patchwork-effect paint scheme. Like the CAG jet, 'Skybolt 623' (BuNo 163525) also participated in *Desert Storm*, flying from the deck of USS *Ranger* (CV 61) with VAQ-131.

Although launch cycles on board the carrier can vary widely in terms of the number of aircraft despatched, one factor always remains constant: the E-2 is the first machine aloft and the last one to recover. Like the remaining elements of CVW-2, VAW-116 'Sun Kings' were flying the very latest spec aircraft available to the Navy on *WestPac 95* in the form of four Group II E-2Cs. Although externally similar to a 'vanilla' C-model Hawkeye, the Group II is a significantly upgraded machine which has had virtually all its sensory systems enhanced. Perhaps the

greatest change centres around the aircraft's Grumman/General Electric APS-145 radar, which has replaced the 1988-vintage APS-139. The former system boasts greater levels of threat detection and processing capability, better overland performance thanks to reduced ground clutter returns, and a greater ability to locate and identify targets at extreme distances. The new Hazeltine APX-100 IFF (Identification Friend or Foe) system and JTIDS (Joint Tactical Information Distribution System) have also further increased the mission effectiveness of

the Hawkeye, while the installation of uprated (by 1,200hp) Allison T56-A-427 turboprop engines has improved the aircraft's flight performance. This power increase means that the Group II E-2C's landing characteristics differ from those of the older Group 0 aircraft, and in order to allow LSOs (Landing Signal Officers) to differentiate between the two externally identical types, and thus give them the correct approach calls when lined up for recovery, a plus symbol has been sprayed on to the aircraft's radome.

The pilot has already activated the wing-fold mechanism on 'Sun King 602' (BuNo 164487) despite the fact that his aircraft is still well and truly snagged in the arrestor wire. Note the prominent blade aerials attached to the underside of the Hawkeye's once smooth fuselage, these having been added to the aircraft as part of its Group II upgrade.

Although this machine (BuNo 164112) was indeed the unit's CAG aircraft, and therefore entitled to wear full squadron colours, all four 'Sun Kings' Hawkeyes were meticulously decorated with maroon and gold detail markings for the duration of *WestPac 95*. This aircraft was still serving as VAW-116's 'CAG bird' in late 1996.

Below:
CVW-2's Prowlers may have looked ready for a rest by the time 'Connie' pulled into Fremantle Harbour, but the wing's S-3Bs appeared fit only for the 'boneyard' at Davis-Monthan. The mottled appearance of 'Griffin 705' (BuNo 160576) was typical of the eight VS-38 Vikings aboard CV 64, these aircraft having flown myriad hours in support of other tactical jets within the air wing during the recently completed Operation *Southern Watch*. While on station off Iraq, the unit performed the dual role of Armed Surface Reconnaissance (ASR) and aerial tanking, the former mission involving the monitoring of Iraqi radar and missile sites with the S-3B's sophisticated suite of ALR-76 ESM sensors, and the latter the use of a Douglas D-704 buddy-buddy underwing pod, as seen fitted to this jet. This particular aircraft had participated in the very last S-3A *WestPac* back in 1992/3 aboard USS *Ranger*, again with VS-38 within CVW-2; it had first visited Western Australia as long ago as January 1983, serving as the CAG jet for VS-37 'Sawbucks' with CVW-11 aboard USS *Enterprise*.

VS-38's CAG jet (BuNo 160573) didn't look a whole lot better than 'Griffin 705', the unit's only concession to its role as *the* premier S-3B within the squadron being the application of the famous 'Red Griffin' in the appropriate shade. Again carrying a refuelling pod on its port stores pylon, this aircraft has also participated in many a *WestPac* cruise during its fifteen plus years of fleet service. Its first Perth port call occurred back in February 1982, again as part of VS-38 on board *Constellation*, but this time controlled by CVW-9.

Above:
No matter from what angle you viewed VS-38's Vikings, their aircraft still looked decidedly second-hand – the leading edge weathering on this jet has even spread to the tail fin and nose radome. Having supported VAQ-131's Prowlers during their war-at-sea exercise both with ASUW (Anti-Surface Unit Warfare) tactics using the jet's advanced Texas Instruments AN/APS-137(V)1 Inverse Synthetic Aperture Radar (ISAR) and in-flight refuelling, 'Griffin 705' lands back on board accompanied by the 'burping' engine noise synonymous with the throttling up and down of the Viking's General Electric TF34-GE-2 turbofans.

Below:
Arms outstretched as a visual cue both to the LSO's platform and the remaining arrestor gear crewmen, a 'green-shirt' signals that the 'wire' has fallen clear of the tailhook on 'Griffin 706' (BuNo 158872). The oldest airframe in VS-38 during *WestPac 95*, this particular Viking was actually the twelfth jet built by Lockheed in the initial production batch of thirteen for the US Navy, authorised in April 1972. Its two previous visits to Perth had been with VS-37 as part of CVW-14 on board 'Connie' in September 1987 and then again with CV 64 in April 1989. The deployable trailing edge single-slot flap fitted to the Viking is clearly visible in this elevated view, the former bestowing upon the aircraft superb low-speed handling characteristics.

For many years the only other Viking variant to share deck space with the ASW-dedicated A-models were the US-3A CODs, all of which were finally retired at the end of 1994. Today, a handful of highly modified ES-3As also regularly deploy in detachment strength with air wings on 'blue water' ops, these jets being flown by crews from VQ-5 'Sea Shadows' on the west coast and VQ-6 'Black Ravens' 'back east'. A typical det for a *WestPac* or *AirLant* cruise of six months' duration comprises two jets, three pilots and three Naval Flight Officers (plus an officer in charge, who is always a pilot or NFO), a maintenance officer, intelligence officer and fifty enlisted personnel – the latter include aircrew who fly, as well as performing regular maintenance tasks. CV 64 welcomed on board VQ-5's 'Det Alpha' for its *WestPac* cruise in 1995, the flight operating ES-3As' 158862 and 159397 – the latter jet is seen here. The VQ units describe their role as providing the 'ears' of the fleet, using highly sophisticated radar and radio direction-

finding equipment to monitor electronic communications across the airwaves. Aside from the new radome and direction-finding antenna fitted in the dorsal fuselage 'shoulder', the ES-3A also bristles with some sixty plus antennae on its fuselage and

wings, all of which combine to make the jet some fifteen per cent heavier than a 'vanilla' S-3B.

The rotary-wing element within CVW-2 was provided by the mixed force of SH-60Fs and HH-60Hs of HS-2 'Golden Hawks'. This unit is the most experienced operator of the 'CV Seahawk' in the US Navy, having received its first helicopters in place of its veteran SH-3H Sea Kings at its NAS North Island home in March 1990. The first *WestPac* undertaken by the squadron commenced in February 1991 when it embarked four SH-60Fs and two

HH-60Hs aboard USS *Nimitz* (CVN 68) as part of CVW-9. HS-2 brought its wealth of Seahawk experience to CVW-2 in late 1992 when the air wing was reorganised in preparation for its first *WestPac* with the newly refitted CV 64. CVW-2's previous rotary-wing squadron, HS-14, exchanged its Sea Kings for Seahawks soon after being replaced by HS-2, and today flies with CVW-5 aboard USS *Independence* CV 62).

Equipped with a 120 US gal external tank on its starboard stores pylon, this HH-60H (BuNo 163792) is undertaking a 'hot crew turnaround' between launch cycles, swapping its four-man crew without its engines being shut down.

The second HH-60H embarked by the squadron on CV 64 in 1995 was BuNo 163793, this machine looking far less weathered than 'Hunter 614'. Many of the

external features which differentiate the HH-60 from the more common SH-60 are visible in this view, including the twin cabin windows on the port side, HIRSS (Hover

Infra-Red Suppressor Subsystem) exhaust suppressors and the Loral AN/ALE-39 chaff/flare dispenser fitted to the right of the toned down 'Old Glory'.

Above :
Working 'up on the roof' is a dirty job, a fact to which the clothing of this youthful 'blue-shirted' 'chock and chain' man graphically attests to. Slung over his shoulder is the ubiquitous rubber wheel chock, literally hundreds of which are deployed across the deck at any one time. Apart from securing the aircraft to the ship when not in use, these guys also operate the tow tractors and 'huffers' (tractors fitted with auxiliary jet starter units).

Above:
Two 'purple-shirted' refuellers put their backs into unrolling JP-5 hoses from the catwalk reels situated on the port side of the deck. The use of these strategically sited

bowsers allows the deck to remain uncluttered with hoses and refuelling equipment. Twenty-six refuelling stations are dotted around the edge of 'Connie's' deck.

Left:
No doubt happy at the thought of hitting the US Navy's favourite *WestPac* R&R port after weeks on station in the Gulf, two ordnance men from VFA-151 take a break from fitting guidance vanes to live Sparrow rounds attached to the XO's Hornet. A close examination of their 'float coats' reveals the marker dye, beacon and manual inflation tube built into each jacket worn on deck; an internal flotation bladder triggered by the wearer's immersion in salt water is built into the lining of each coat.

Below:
The cat officer 'hits the deck' and signals to the shooter (visible over his left shoulder with his hands in the air) to press the fire button for bow cat four. This is the final act in a complex, but nevertheless speedy, performance that has seen the aircraft attached to the launch shuttle, power and flight controls checked and catapult pressure set to match the jet's weight – all without a word being exchanged between air- and deckcrew.

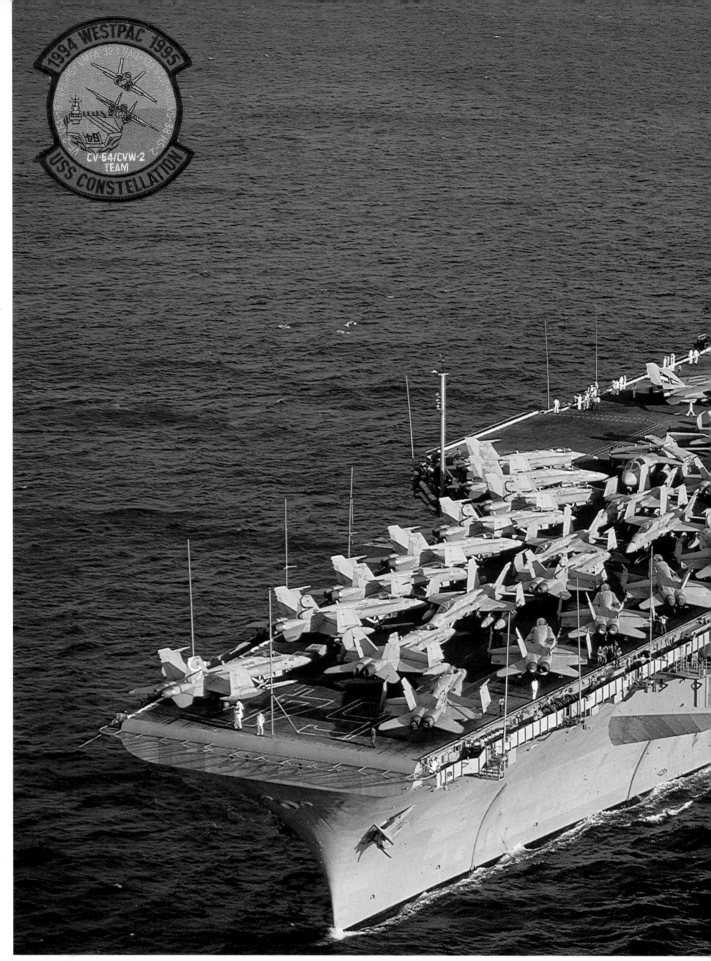

This spread and overleaf:
After seventy-three days 'on the line' deep in the Persian Gulf, CV 64 and her crew of 5,000-plus were rewarded with near consecutive port calls to Fremantle and Sydney in early April 1995. As is standard practice for any visit to a foreign port, the crew lined the catwalk in full dress uniform (white for summer, blue for winter), and various welcoming signal flags were run up the ship's mast. The hangar deck was 'cleared out' as much as possible, leaving only twelve airframes undercover. No fewer than sixty-two machines can be seen in these aerial views taken from a Kawasaki-Bell KH-4 on the morning of 8 April 1995.

Below:
The island dominates the flightdeck of any 'supercarrier', and 'Connie' is no exception. The central mast towering out from above the superstructure is festooned with various air and surface search antennae and satcomm receivers. It is topped by the flat TACAN antenna, some 200ft above the waterline. The secondary tower aft of the island supports the radar dish for the AN/SPS-48 aircraft control system, while the various white domes house direction-finding antennae.

The 28mm wide-angle lens fitted to the camera exaggerates the length of the carrier. Known as 'America's Flagship', CV 64 is some 1,079ft long and 270ft wide, and tips the scales at 88,000 tons when loaded to combat displacement. Her initial cost to the US taxpayer was $400 million in 1961, but the vessel's three-year SLEP, completed in 1993, totalled $800 million. She was commanded on *WestPac 95* by Capt. Marc A Ostertag, an ex-fighter pilot with 4,000-plus hours on F-8s, F-4s and F-14s. Among his previous postings was a spell as XO on board USS *John F Kennedy* (CV 67).

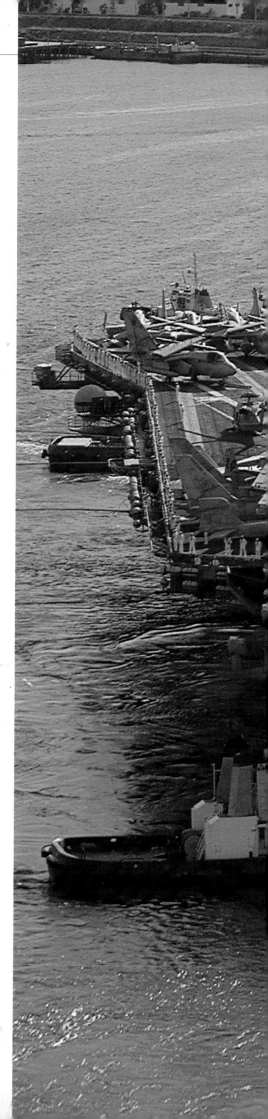

Previous page:
Fremantle Port Authority (FPA) tugs gently nudge CV 64 towards its berthing alongside the harbour's passenger terminal. For many years 'supercarriers' were forced to moor in Gage Roads, some one to two miles off shore, because the draught of the inner harbour was too shallow to accommodate these vessels. However, in the late 1980s the FPA undertook an extensive dredging programme that meant from 1989 onwards conventionally powered carriers could berth inside the harbour itself, easing the comings and goings of the crew during their five-day R&R period and streamlining victualling.

Inset:
The stern of the carrier becomes 'fighter town' during a port visit, with deck handlers positioning Tomcats nose to tail in order to make optimum use of the room available. The wing oversweep mechanism built into the F-14 by Grumman is used to great effect during spells of R&R, the flying surface being cranked back past the 68° position attainable in flight.

No fewer than twenty-two of the thirty-six Lot XV F/A-18Cs embarked on 'Connie' crowd the bow of the carrier (an area known as 'Four Row'). This is a graphic demonstration of just how close experienced deck marshallers can spot aircraft next to each other. Note how each Hornet unit has adopted a different colour for its respective jet nozzle covers.

'Big John'

Date: July 1996
Location: English Channel
Aircraft Carrier: USS *John F Kennedy* (CV 67)

By the time *Constellation* finally sailed into the Delaware River at the completion of its SLEP in the spring of 1993, its dry-dock 'home' within the huge Philadelphia Naval Yard was hastily being made ready for its next 'customer' desperate for a 'face-lift' to see it safely through to the 21st century. That vessel was 'Connie's' younger *Kitty Hawk*-class sister-ship USS *John F Kennedy* (CV 67), a veteran of the Gulf War and numerous *NorLant* deployments with the Sixth Fleet. Like CV 64, 'Big John' had been scheduled to undergo a complete three-year overhaul, but with ever-shrinking defence budgets emerging from Capitol Hill, the US Navy decided to cut short the carrier's rework programme and pull her out of dry-dock in September 1995, a full year ahead of the original completion date. The result of this curtailed refit was a reduced service life extension of between five to eight years, rather than the ten to twelve bestowed upon 'Connie'.

With CV 67 declared available to the Navy once again, the carrier changed home ports from Norfolk to Mayport, in Florida. Soon after returning to the frontline, 'JFK' was designated as the new reserve carrier in place of the now mothballed USS *Forrestal* (CV 59). While fulfilling this role, 'JFK's' refurbished deck played host to the TA-4Js of Training Air Wing 1 and VT-7, which completed a CNATra (Chief, Naval Aviation Training) carrier qualification detachment in November 1995. That same month the F/A-18A-equipped VFA-204 became the first reserve unit to become carqualled on board its newly designated 'floating home', operating from the carrier's angled deck for several days while the vessel sailed off the Florida coast.

Unlike its predecessor in the reserve-affiliated role, 'Big John' has retained its full weapons suite and state-of-the-art sensor and fighter control systems to allow it to remain very much in the frontline. Further proof of its active fleet tasking came with the announcement that CVW-8 was to be assigned to CV 67, this air wing having recently returned from an eventful Mediterranean cruise that had seen its aircraft fly in support of Operations *Southern Watch, Deny Flight* and *Deliberate Force* from the deck of USS *Theodore Roosevelt* (CVN 71); the air wing had also completed a brief shakedown cruise with the Navy's newest carrier, the USS *John C Stennis* (CVN 74), as recently as December 1995.

The first major deployment undertaken by 'JFK' commenced on 17 May 1996 when the vessel welcomed on board CVW-8 for a six-week *NorLant* 'mini' cruise to the Republic of Ireland and England. This trip would act as an early shakedown for both the carrier and the air wing in preparation for a fully blown six-month deployment commencing in April 1997. After spending the first three days of the

Union flag fluttering in the breeze in deference to its hosts, 'JFK' makes for an impressive sight off the Hampshire coast. Pulled out of the Philadelphia Naval Shipyard in the late autumn of 1995 to fill the gap left by the now retired USS *America* (CV 66), CV 67 has reaped the benefits of expenditure that reputedly topped the $300 million mark while in refit. Although not enjoying a fully blown SLEP like semi-sister-ships *Kitty Hawk* and *Constellation*, 'Big John's' rework should guarantee its place in the active fleet inventory for another six to eight years.

trip carrying out day and night carquals in the VaCapes OpArea, the air wing shifted to more conventional cyclic ops as the carrier steered a course for the Republic of Ireland. Reflecting the unique nature of this deployment, CVW-8 comprised two Tomcat and two Hornet squadrons, rather than the more typical one-to-three split of the modern air wing – the embarked EW, AWACS and ASW assets remained the same as usual, however. This fighter-biased make-up allowed VFs -14 and -41 and VFAs -15 and -87 to generate some impressive mixed section sorties in both air-to-air and air-to-ground modes during the transatlantic crossing.

The highlight of the brief shakedown deployment was the vessel's visit to Dublin, where it formed the centrepiece of the anniversary celebrations staged by the Irish Navy – rumour also has it that the US Ambassador to Ireland, Jean Kennedy-Smith (the late John F Kennedy's sister, no less), may have had a say in the vessel's sailing schedule. So great was the demand made by the local populace to visit 'their' carrier (CV 67's crest has a strong Irish flavour to it, reflecting its namesake's Gaelic ancestry) that 10,000 tickets assuring the holder a tour on board were issued via Ireland's national lottery.

While the sheer physical presence of the 80,000-ton carrier clearly 'stole the show' during its Irish stay, elements of the vessel's embarked air wing came into their own soon after 'JFK' had weighed anchor by putting up a sixteen-strong formation that comprised four F-14As (two each from both VFs -14 and -41), six F/A-18Cs (two from VFA-15 and four from VFA-87), two E-2Cs from VAW-124, and four S-3Bs from VS-24. These jets overflew both Dublin and Cork as a final 'thank you' gesture to their generous hosts, before heading east across the Irish Sea (refuelled en route by

Above:
Reflecting the general maintenance period observed by CVW-8 during the Portsmouth visit, 'Ace 110' (BuNo 162603, delivered to the Navy in December 1985) has its M61A1 Vulcan cannon and associated 675-round drum serviced just forward of the carrier's number four elevator. The weapons pallet fitted beneath the jet's centrebody has also been winched down to ease access to the F-14A's internal systems. Note the ejector racks fitted to the pallet, an external store which featured on virtually all the Tomcats on board 'JFK', thus turning them into 'Bombcats'. VF-41 created history during Operation *Deliberate Force* over Bosnia when two laser-munitions-equipped F-14As from the unit became the first Tomcats to drop live ordnance in action when they bombed Serbian targets on 5 September 1995. The 'Black Aces' went on to deliver 24,000lb of precision-guided ordnance during a solid week of bombing in conjunction with laser-equipped F/A-18Cs from VFAs -15 and -87.

Lighters and Royal Navy tugs bustle around 'Big John' soon after the vessel had dropped anchor in the Solent. As is common practice in the US Navy, the fighter community spotted the majority of its jets aft, which left the remaining deck area free for the smaller types within the air wing. The sole E-2C clearly stands out in a sea of uniform grey due to the lighter, more glossy shade of its finish, complete with full colour/full size 'stars and bars'. The yellow vertical bar affixed to the stern of the carrier is part of a series of landing lights that line up with the centreline of the angled deck, thus providing a crucial visual cue for approaching aircraft. The white-faced rectangular box that breaks the bar two thirds of the way up is the azimuth dome for the SPS-41 Automatic Carrier Landing System (ACLS); the elevation dome for this crucial piece of equipment is mounted on a platform some fifteen feet up from the base of the lattice mast, astern of the island. This system has been replaced on CV 64 by Laser Guidance Inc's Laser Centerline Localizer (LCL) and Laser Glidescope Indicator (LGI), which have proved suitable for precision approaches in the darkest of weather out to distances of twenty miles. Laser Visual Landing Aids (LVLA) utilise low-power/eye-safe lasers to provide visual 'needles' in the form of two balls of light below the roundown (the LCL) and on the island, abaft the LLD 'meatball'. It is proposed that this system will eventually be fitted to all frontline carriers.

the S-3Bs) with the intention of recovering back on board their carrier. However, some seventy miles off the south-west coast of England, 'JFK' sailed into fog so thick that even the plane-guard HH-60 found it difficult to land back on board. Faced with little option but to land ashore at a secured military facility, the aircraft quickly altered their flight plan and recovered en masse at RNAS Yeovilton, in Somerset, much to the delight of the naval air station's airshow organisers, who were staging their annual event that weekend (13/14 July). Further elements of CVW-8 in the shape of a pair of SH-60Fs and a solitary S-3B spent time on shore at Boulmer during 'JFK's' four-day visit to Portsmouth.

The latter port call was a low-key affair when compared with the Dublin visit, the air wing's maintenance crews using the time to carry out rectification work on a number of jets prior to the carrier

It is debatable whether the famous 'high hat' emblem of VF-14 will grace the deck of 'JFK' next time the carrier steams into European waters, as CVW-8 is likely to deploy with just a single Tomcat squadron on board for a proper Sixth Fleet cruise, thus bringing its composition into line with virtually all other frontline air wings. However, during *NorLant 96* VF-14 was numerically the larger of the two fighter squadrons embarked, its complement of ten F-14As reflecting its added TARPS role. The seventeen-strong Tomcat force embarked for the 1996 mini-cruise featured some of the longest-serving F-14s still flying in the fleet, with two of VF-14's jets ('Tophatter's' '212'/BuNo 158615 and '216'/BuNo 158617) being the oldest aircraft in the entire frontline fighter community – both were part of the initial Block 60 order for eight aircraft delivered by Grumman back in late 1972.

The personal mount of VFA-15's XO, Cdr Mark 'Guad' Guadagnini, 'Valion 302' (BuNo 164643) has the panel covering its port avionics equipment bay hinged open for a series of 'black box' checks. Operating Lot XIV night attack capable F/A-18Cs, the 'Valions' made full use of their jets during round-the-clock strikes on Bosnian Serb targets in August/September 1995. Over fifty sorties were flown by the unit, who successfully hit ammunition dumps and military lines of communication; forty-seven LGBs, nine AGM-88s, two SLAM and three GBU-24 Hard Target Penetrators (the first to be used in combat by the US Navy) were expended during fourteen days of flying. The unit also completed seventy Suppression of Enemy Air Defence (SEAD) sorties during this period.

sailing back into the Atlantic for its two-week passage to Florida. Exercises in the Caribbean rounded out the *NorLant,* and CV 67 and CVW-8 parted company until commencing carquals and work-ups later in 1996.

This VFA-87 jet ('Warrior 406'/BuNo 164644) is seen just prior to engine runs being performed on its twin General Electric F404-GE-400 turbofans while securely chained to the deck. Note the presence of no fewer than five 330 US gal tanks – the store on the extreme left has been adorned with a full-colour VFA-87 spear, denoting its previous use by the unit's CAG aircraft. VFA-87 had no designated 'CAG bird' embarked during *NorLant 96,* deploying with eight rather than a full cruise complement of twelve jets.

Embarked Aircraft

VF-41 'Black Aces' – F-14A Tomcat

160893/103	160407/106	162603/110	160926/112
161161/113	161134/114	160391/120	

VF-14 'Tophatters' – F-14A Tomcat

160687/200	159863/201	162689/203	160411/207
160908/210	158615/212	160396/213	162688/214
159848/215	158617/216		

VFA-15 'Valions' – F/A-18C Hornet

164627/300	164629/301	164643/302	164646/303
164655/304	164680/311	164631/312	164678/314

VFA-87 'Golden Warriors' – F/A-18C Hornet

164675/401	164647/402	164663/403	164657/405
164644/406	164668/407	164630/412	164628/414

VAW-124 'Bear Aces' – E-2C Hawkeye

163026/600	161099/601	162799/602

HS-3 'Trident' – SH-60F/HH-60H Seahawk
SH-60F

164450/610	164451/611	164454/612	164455/613
164099/617			

HH-60H

165115/614	165116/615

VAQ-141 'Shadowhawks' – EA-6B Prowler

163526/621	163049/622	163530/623

VS-24 'Scouts' – S-3B Viking

158873/700	158866/701	160142/702	159741/704
159744/706	160153/707		

One of the most heavily utilised assets in the US military arsenal of the 1990s is the EA-6B Prowler, its mission taskings continuing to increase disproportionately to its fleet strength as we approach the millennium. Perhaps as an indication of the finite number of hours left on Prowler airframes in the fleet, none of VAQ-141's trio of EA-6Bs embarked on 'JFK' participated in the Dublin/Cork flypast. This jet ('Desperado 623'/BuNo 163530) wears single mobile SAM radar and miniature AGM-88 HARM symbols beneath its Modex, denoting its successful participation in Operation *Dead-Eye Southeast* – the crippling of the Bosnian Serb integrated air defence network in August/September 1995 during Operation *Deliberate Force*. VAQ-141 assets were split between *Theodore Roosevelt* (with the rest of CVW-8) and Aviano air base, in Italy, during the conflict.

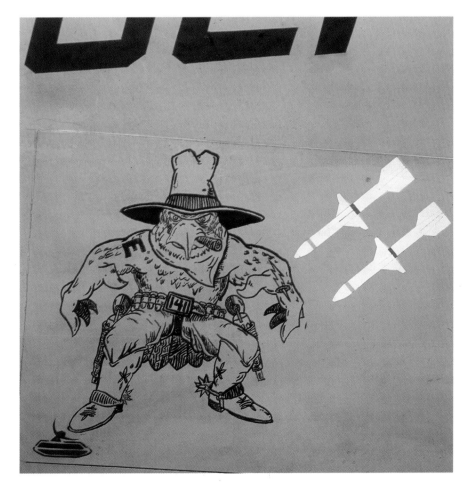

This neat piece of nose art, seen on 'Desperado 621' (BuNo 163526), features two AGM-88s, a mobile SAM radar, and a 'gunslinging' 'Shadowhawk', symbol of VAQ-141 – note the 'Battle E', awarded for sustained efficiency in the frontline, on the bird's right shoulder, the '141' titling on its belt buckle, and EW lightning bolt on its left forearm. Like BuNo 163530, this jet flew from the deck of *Theodore Roosevelt* during *Deliberate Force*.

A single red lightning bolt was the extent of the rather muted unit markings worn on VS-24's S-3B Vikings, although a number of jets wore *SCOUT FUEL* titling on the external refuelling pods. The 'Scouts', who can trace their history back to Bombing Squadron 17 (established on 1 January 1943), have performed the ASW role since April 1950. Boasting an impressive record of accident-free flying that stretches back twelve years, VS-24 was re-rolled as a Sea Control Squadron in 1993, although it still retains the traditional ASW designation. 'Scout 706' (BuNo 159744) had only recently

been reissued to VS-24 prior to the deployment commencing following a lengthy Naval Air Rework Facility (NARF) overhaul – hence its near pristine finish when compared with other 'Scouts' S-3Bs. During the unit's last Sixth Fleet deployment in 1995 it too was heavily involved in *Deliberate Force*, flying armed surface recce,

electronic strike support, and aerial refuelling sorties. One of its S-3Bs also became the first frontline Viking to launch four Tactical Air Launched Decoys (TALDs) in a single sortie, this remarkable effort being performed in support of a joint F/A-18C/EA-6B strike on Serbian radar and SAM targets in eastern Bosnia.

Right:
The sole E-2C on board 'JFK' during her visit to Portsmouth was sixteen-year-old Group 0 machine BuNo 161099, and like sister Hawkeye BuNo 162799 ('602') deployed to Yeovilton for the duration of the port call, this aircraft had served with VAW-123 'Screwtops' until just prior to joining VAW-124 for *NorLant 96*. Its former owner's distinctive 'swirl' atop the Randtron APN-71 antenna rotodome had been crudely painted out on this E-2.

Opposite:
Sitting side by side in the shadow of CV 67's island, 'Troubleshooters 612' (BuNo 164454) and '613' (BuNo 164455) of HSL-3 'Tridents' followed each other down the Sikorsky SH-60F production line in 1992. Both helicopters are seen here identically configured right down to the trident-adorned external fuel tanks. The first Atlantic Fleet squadron to

receive the 'CV Seahawk' in place of the venerable SH-3H Sea King back in August 1991, HSL-3 transferred from CVW-17 to CVW-8 in the process. The 'Tridents' were the only unit within CVW-8 to embark on 'Big John' for *NorLant 96* in full squadron strength – five SH-60Fs and two HH-60Hs participated in the deployment.

CVW-2 Work-ups

Date: October 1996
Location: Pacific Ocean
Aircraft Carrier: USS *Constellation* (CV 64)

Illustrating the significant changes that have taken place in US Navy colour schemes in the F-14's lifetime, 'Bullets 101' (BuNo 159630) and '115' (BuNo 159600) share ramp space immediately astern of CV 64's island during operations in the SoCal OpArea in late October 1996. The eighteenth, and last, F-14D(R) rebuilt by Northrop Grumman, 'Bullet 101' was reissued to VF-2 in late 1995 following its respray by the manufacturer in a $90,000 paint scheme to mark the twenty-fifth anniversary of the YF-14A's first flight on 21 December 1970; having operated the Tomcat longer than any other frontline unit, it was fitting that VF-2 should be chosen to supply the commemorative aircraft. The scheme chosen was that originally adopted by the 'Bounty Hunters' when their first A-models arrived at NAS Miramar in July 1973, to which was added two twenty-fifth anniversary logos on the inside of each fin. Research for the special paint job was undertaken by the then VF-2 maintenance officer (and RIO) Lt-Cdr Tom 'Tumor' Twomey, and the only area in which the 'new' jet differed from a 1973-vintage machine was in the former lacking gloss white overwing spoilers. Both these Tomcats originally entered service with the Navy as A-models in late 1975.

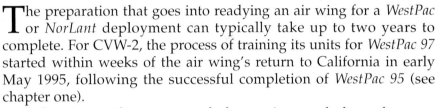

The preparation that goes into readying an air wing for a *WestPac* or *NorLant* deployment can typically take up to two years to complete. For CVW-2, the process of training its units for *WestPac 97* started within weeks of the air wing's return to California in early May 1995, following the successful completion of *WestPac 95* (see chapter one).

After six months at sea, regularly carrying out deck ops for up to sixteen hours a day, seven days a week, aircrewmen are operating at peak performance in terms of both the efficiency in which they complete a mission tasking and the way they handle their aircraft 'around the boat'. They are ably supported in their endeavours by the technical personnel assigned to the unit back on the ship, who strive to keep sophisticated combat aircraft serviceable in arguably the world's most hostile environment. The fact that maintainers achieve this task is proved in sortie completion rates that hover around the 100 per cent mark for months on end.

Maintaining this mission proficiency once the air wing has broken up into component units following the carrier's return to its home port is a hard task made all the more difficult by the fact that drastic changes in personnel usually occur within months of the squadrons returning to their respective air stations. Typically, more than half of the squadrons' cruise complement of aircrew will be posted away to other units where they can impart their recently acquired knowledge to nugget 'naval aviators' who are in the process of training for future 'blue water' ops. Their place in the frontline is in turn taken by a mix of 'JOs' (Junior Officers) and single tour veterans, the latter usually returning to the frontline having finished a stint at a training unit or 'flying a desk' in an administrative role. The squadron boss also invariably leaves soon after the deployment has ended, his XO from the previous cruise assuming command of the unit and proceeding to build it back up to strength in preparation for the next *WestPac* or *NorLant* sailing. For new pilots on the squadron, the route to achieving mission-capable status usually follows a set syllabus mapped out by experienced NavAir instructors for the aircraft type in question, interspersed with unique unit-generated operational taskings that tailor the 'finished product' to the needs of that particular outfit. An example of the latter within CVW-2 is provided by Marine-manned VMFA-323 which, although essentially performing the light strike role in conjunction with fellow F/A-18C-equipped squadrons VFAs -137 and -151, also specialises in the Close Air Support mission as befits a USMC unit.

Although ostensibly shore-based for much of the time between

Almost as colourful as BuNo 159630, 'Bullet 100' (BuNo 163895) was in fact painted in the overall darker shade of TPS grey reserved usually for CAG jets within the Tomcat community. Seen in chapter one wearing the red, white and blue 'Langley stripe' on its twin fins, the aircraft was restored to a near authentic 1973 finish in September 1995 in order to serve as a backdrop for VF-2's change of command ceremony at Miramar at which present CO, Cdr Lawrence S Rice, relieved Cdr L Scott Lamoreaux. Sadly, the latter was killed on 18 February 1996 when the VF-11 F-14D he was flying in suffered a catastrophic engine fire and literally blew up over the Pacific off California during a simulated anti-ship missile profile staged as part of USS *Carl Vinson's* (CVN 70) CompTuEx. Having been called in to land from its pre-designated orbit at 3,000ft, 'Bullet 100' vents fuel in order to achieve its desired landing weight as it leads '106' down the starboard side of the carrier.

six-month deployments, elements of the air wing will still operate with and against 'blue water' assets as part of their work-up. For CVW-2, this involved supporting USS Carl Vinson's (CVN 70) battle group, which was completing a demanding extended CompTuEx/ITA (Competitive Training Unit Exercise/Intermediate Training Assessment) and Joint Task Force Exercise. The first prolonged at-sea period for CVW-2/CV 64 then followed with a mini-cruise up the west coast to Canada, which allowed new pilots within the air wing to get carqualled. Once back on shore, individual units participated in various exercises independently of the air wing. An example of this was VFA-151's three-week-long visit to Tucson International Airport for air-to-air training with the F-16-equipped 162nd Fighter Wing of the Arizona Air National Guard. Just prior to that, the unit had successfully passed its annual conventional weapons technical proficiency inspection, thus getting another 'tick in the box' on its way to achieving full mission readiness for WestPac 97.

Meanwhile, at NAS Miramar VF-2 was also excelling in its chosen field, winning the prestigious (and last) West Coast Fighter Derby, an annual competition which pitted all frontline Tomcats squadrons against one another to see who was the best at performing the jet's demanding fleet defence role. It also won the 'recce rally' for TARPS-equipped units and the Phoenix missile

With sufficient JP-5 having been dumped, 'Bullet 100' powers on over the roundown, heading for a three-wire recovery. Fitted snugly between its 280 US gal external tanks is a TARPS (Tactical Air Reconnaissance Pod System) pod, this hefty 1,750lb external store being affixed to weapon station five – landing weights become super-critical with a TARPS-equipped Tomcat. Using a modified fuel tank to house its two cameras (KS-87B frame camera in the nose of the pod and a KA-99/KA-93 panoramic camera or KS-153A frame camera), infra-red reconnaissance set (AN/AAD-5) and data display system (AN/ASQ-172), the TARPS has proven so effective since being issued to the fleet in 1981 that its status as an interim recce fix until the stillborn RF-18A could enter service has long since been upgraded to a permanent fit. Fewer than seventy A-model Tomcats were modified to carry TARPS, which usually meant just three airframes could be issued to a frontline unit at any one time. However, with the retirement of a considerable number of Tomcats over the past five years, the ratio of recce jets to 'vanilla' airframes has increased – all F-14Ds (both new and upgraded) can carry TARPS.

Mission over, the TARPS is carefully removed from the stores pylon by VF-2's dedicated 'recce techs', prior to 'Bullet 100' being re-configured for an up and coming bombing sortie. For many years only a handful of experienced crews within a Tomcat squadron would be cleared for the TARPS mission principally because of the pod's adverse effect on the jet's recovery characteristics. However, with the onus now on squadrons to train up crews for the TARPS role in-house, rather than the RAG performing this function ashore, all flying personnel within VF-2 are currently being instructed in the art of aerial recce. Despite this opening up of the tasking squadron wide, the D-model jet can still be a handful on recovery, particularly on a still day on board a conventional carrier – critical wind speeds over the deck have to be reached to allow the heavy jet to land safely, as the TARPS Tomcat has to recover 'long' in order to ensure that the pod does not strike the deck on touchdown. Conventional carriers can sometimes struggle to attain the thirty knots-plus speeds needed on windless days, whereas CVNs rarely have any trouble attaining such a figure.

award. In the summer of 1996 the unit moved to NAS Oceana, Virginia, as part of the Navy's reorganisation of the ever-shrinking fighter community. Soon after arriving on the east coast, VF-2 showed its prowess in its new-found fighter-bomber role by winning a mid-Atlantic strike competition against stiff opposition – five other Tomcat units and ten F/A-18C squadrons, plus teams from the USMC's AV-8B Harrier II community.

The S-3B-equipped VS-38 was also kept busy during this period with a variety of ASW exercises that saw it operating with Australian, Canadian and Chilean assets, as well as US Navy vessels. Indeed, the unit provided detachments of aircraft both to a Canadian Armed Forces base and a Chilean naval air station during this work-up phase, the latter proving particularly challenging as some of the mission taskings undertaken involved 800-mile round trips on surface warfare strikes against Chilean fast missile patrol boats. Further emphasising the all-round capability of the S-3B, VS-38 then went on to qualify twenty-four aircrewmen in weapons delivery tactics over the bombing ranges at NAF El Centro, California, employing 500, 1,000 and 2,000lb Mk 80 freefall and Snakeye retarded bombs.

Having operated very much apart for most of the summer months, the component units within CVW-2 finally came together in August/September for a STRIKE det to NAS Fallon, Nevada, where air wing tactics were firstly formulated, and then put to the test. With the successful completion of the most realistic peacetime combat training course on offer to any air arm in the world, CVW-2 'hit the boat' in mid-October to complete three weeks of training in the SoCal Ops area off the southern California coast. During this period the progress made by the nine units that comprised the air

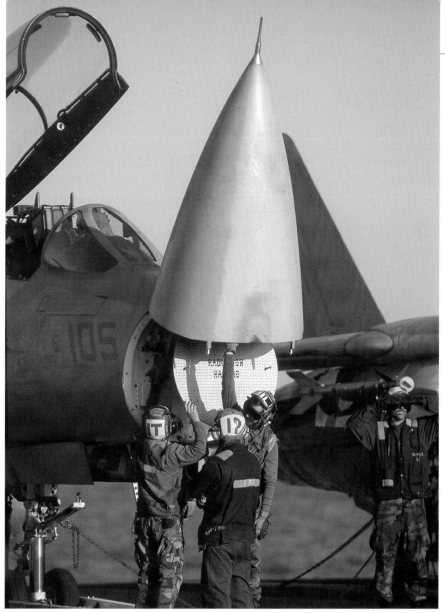

The upgraded 'eyes' of the D-model undergo a quick visual check prior to the start of the day's flying. The AN/APG-71 radar is effectively a digitalised version of the tried and tested Hughes AN/AWG-9, arguably the most powerful western air intercept radar to see widespread frontline service. In addition to digitalisation, the new radar has been linked with dual multibus AYK-14 processors, which make the avionics fit more versatile when it comes to performing other roles. Despite the undoubted superiority of the AN/APG-71 over its predecessor, the former is not entirely suited to precision ground attack work as former Intruder pilot Lt Curt Seth explains: 'The A-6E was more versatile as a bomb dropper thanks to its FLIR, TRAM and AN/APQ-156 air-to-ground radar, but was hindered by its Vietnam era flight systems. My F-14D, on the other hand, has state-of-the-art avionics and flight systems, but lacks a suitable air-to-ground mode in the AN/APG-71. However, we will soon be getting a LANTIRN pod and FLIR, and this will greatly enhance our ability to deliver PGMs [Precision-Guided Munitions].'

A 'huffer' takes the strain as 'Bullet 114' (BuNo 159628) is towed aft over the arrestor wires for respotting on the fantail of CV 64 at the end of a cycle of ops. Note that the tractor driver has a whistle clenched between his teeth, which he will use to warn other bodies on the deck of his presence. This jet was one of six F-14D(R)s embarked on the carrier for the October work-up period.

wing could be accurately gauged, for they performed typical *WestPac* taskings against various bombing ranges, subsurface and surface targets and aerial threats. VF-2 F-14D pilot Lt Curt Seth explains:

'There are a lot of checks and tests that we have to pass out here to ensure that the air wing, the carrier and the overall battle group are all in agreement in the way that various mission taskings are prosecuted. We are essentially learning to work as a team during this mini-cruise, and the successful completion of this deployment will indicate that we are ready to undertake a *WestPac*.

'Aside from this cruise showing that we can handle our operational taskings, we also have to demonstrate an ability to function effectively aboard "the boat". This means having a sufficient number of serviceable jets available to undertake near round-the-clock operations as all crews attempt to gain mission capable status. We place a heavy demand on our maintenance department, who strive to have a workable stock of Tomcats serviceable for us to use – the demand is arguably higher during this work-up phase than at any time on *WestPac*. Friction can sometimes be generated between the maintenance people and the operations staff on the squadron when the demand for jets means pulling aircraft up from the hangar deck when perhaps the technical people would have liked more time to work on the airframe. Finding effective solutions to these everyday problems is equally as important an aspect of daily operational procedure as prosecuting a

US Navy jets rarely come more blotchy than 'Bullet 112' (BuNo 159619), seen here taxiing forward with its wings in oversweep towards bow cat one. This Tomcat celebrated its twenty-first birthday during CVW-2's SoCal exercise period. The areas of light grey overspray reflect the maintenance work carried out on the aircraft both in the hangar deck and back at NAS Oceana. The application of paint to panel areas (turn screws and latches are invariably chipped while being opened and closed) after rectification work has been completed is considered to be a major 'weapon' in the ongoing fight against metal corrosion.

Squatting precariously beneath the nose of 'Bullet 106' (BuNo 163897), the 'green-shirted' hook-up man signals to the 'shooter' to raise the tension of the catapult to its pre-set value in readiness for launch. A few feet above him, the pilot and RIO keep a keen eye on both the aircraft director up ahead of them and the catapult officer standing away to their left.

potential aerial threat when out on CAP some distance from the carrier.'

For ex-A-6E 'driver' Seth, who was working up towards his third *WestPac* in five years, this frenetic pre-cruise at sea period held few surprises, but for 'nugget' junior officer Lt(jg) Hal 'Bull' Schmitt of VFA-137, this was his first taste of life at 'the pointy end of the stick'. This cruise had come just four-and-a-half months into his tour with the 'Kestrels', and he was finding the increased workload challenging:

'The flying is much as I expected it to be, but the amount of paperwork that has to be done between sorties in order to keep the squadron functioning on a daily basis is quite shocking. I have three administrative jobs to perform aside from my primary function as a Hornet pilot, and I will retain these responsibilities throughout the *WestPac*. There are ten of us junior pilots within the overall squadron complement of eighteen to twenty aircrew, and we are all rapidly acclimatising to life at sea. This is what we have been working towards since entering the Navy three-and-a-half years ago, and our training has been fashioned so that we achieve peak flying performance in time to cope with sustained deck ops at sea as part of an air wing. Because the work-ups in preparation for "hitting the boat" take up so much of your time, the administrative part of the job is occasionally neglected when ashore, and it only really strikes home once you are at sea just how energy-sapping the paperwork can be – at least to start off with.

'Once in the jet, however, the thought of pen pushing is

A 'troubleshooting' safety crewman from VF-2 braces himself for the jet wash expelled from a bomb-laden F-14D stroking down waist cat three. The aircraft will reach 150 knots by the time it leaves the catapult 300ft down the deck, some two seconds after the launch button is pressed by the 'shooter'. The D-model is cleared for non-afterburner launches only, the aircraft's twin General Electric F110-GE-400s being capable of propelling a fully laden Tomcat away from the carrier in military-rated power. The A-model required Zone Three afterburner to achieve a deck take-off.

blocked out and you focus totally on the job at hand. The difference for me between this particular det, and my time say with the Hornet FRS [Fleet Replacement Squadron] at sea, is that the deck crews marshalling you around the "boat", both before and after the mission, expect you to know what you're doing "up on the roof" without having to nursemaid you. In the FRS, they would walk you through the procedure step by step at a slow pace, but here, with a full air wing operating as if "on the line" in the Gulf, there is no time to be watching out for "JOs" finding their feet.

'From a personal point of view, my sole aims for this at sea period are simple – to be able to get off the ship safely at launch and then recover at the completion of my mission in a consistently safe manner. I've only got about thirty-five or so traps to my name at the moment, so I am keen to increase my experience of deck ops as much as possible while aboard. Once I am happy with my performance I can then start to work some of the mission specific stuff while in the air. The latter part of my job was exhaustively addressed during our recent STRIKE det to NAS Fallon, which means that you are pretty familiar with the offensive capabilities of your jet by the time you "hit the boat". It is the blending together of the two aspects of carrier aviation that I am trying to achieve now, and it is a process that is being repeated within the remaining eight units that comprise the air wing.

'Fortunately for me here in VFA-137 we still have a large number of senior lieutenants attached to the unit who have completed *WestPacs* in the past, and they are easily approachable if you have a problem with some aspect of the job. These guys will all be gone before we head out on cruise next spring, but by that stage the "JOs" should be proficient enough to fill the void left by their departure.'

For 'first timers' like Hal Schmitt, achieving the personal goal of mission proficiency is the reward for a successful at-sea period. He has little time to see how his fellow pilots are progressing along the

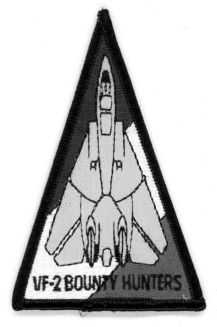

'Bullet 102' (BuNo 164602) climbs away on sheer 'GE power' as the pilot eases back on the stick and prepares to cycle away the flaps and undercarriage before their extended limiting speeds (225 and 280 knots respectively) are exceeded. Note the maximum deflection angle of the all-moving tailplanes.

Right:
Pilot and RIO wait patiently on the deck while their mount ('Bullet 100') is brought up to the flightdeck on elevator four. Both are zippered and buttoned up in full flying gear, comprising a G-suit, parachute harness and survival vest, topped off with a suitably customised flying helmet. Lt Curt Seth again: 'there are seventeen two-man crews in VF-2, and we pair up for a four- to six-month period, which allows us to become familiar with each other's operational characteristics. This familiarity also helps reduce the admin aspect of the pre-flight brief, thus allowing us to concentrate on talking straight tactics. Junior guys are encouraged to pair up with "old heads" so as to spread the wealth of operational experience throughout the squadron.'

Below:
'Connie's' island reflecting in his visor, the RIO completes his deck-level pre-flight check of 'his' jet prior to clambering on board. The video cassette in his hand will record the imagery generated by the undernose Northrop TCS when activated in flight just as a conventional VCR would tape a television signal. This will prove invaluable when debriefing any air combat that may take place during the sortie. Lt Curt Seth: 'Training is becoming a lot tougher for crews in the Tomcat community because of the need to practise fighter, strike, recce and FAC-A [Forward Air Control] taskings. Air-to-air, bomb drops, NVG strikes and LANTIRN all need to be worked up thoroughly for the squadron to be effective in these roles. On the face of it, it would seem that we need to fly more to cope with our greatly expanded mission within the air wing. However, with no more flying hours available, what we are doing is utilising our time more effectively by flying both fighter and strike, or recce and FAC-A, profiles in the same mission.'

same course syllabus, or how the squadron is contributing to the overall effectiveness of the air wing. However, for one pilot within the unit, the latter aspects of the job easily outweigh any personal milestones like 1,000 carrier traps or 2,500 flying hours on a single fast jet type. He is responsible for all 230-plus men (both junior and senior) that comprise the squadron, and has to answer directly to the Commander Air Group in respect to the effectiveness of these sailors. That man is, of course, the squadron's commanding officer.

At the head of VFA-151 is Cdr Dave 'Deke' Philman, a veteran of three *WestPacs* in the A-7E and a single cruise as XO of his current command in F/A-18Cs. His views on the October/November 1996 'mini-cruise' on board CV 64 were most illuminating:

'This deployment is essentially the second at-sea period for the air wing in preparation for the next *WestPac*. To explain its relevance in relation to our impending 1997 cruise, let me regress to the end of the last deployment in May 1995. When we returned to Lemoore after six months away, we were staffed by a group of very mature pilots and maintainers. It is crucial in the overall cycle of things to allow these guys to go from sea to shore duty so as to pass on their experience to new sailors just entering the system. The departure of these individuals essentially means that you have "shut down the railroad". You then go and "hire" a whole bunch of new guys and the work-up cycle starts all over again.

'One of the first major steps in this process is the two-week SFARP [Strike-Fighter Advanced Readiness Program] up at Fallon, which is conducted at squadron level so that we can learn how to perform the basics in a combat environment. This will be followed by a short at-sea period in which the pilots will be carrier qualified for both day and night operations. After a spell back ashore tending the jets in the aftermath of a punishing "blue water" cycle of ops, the air wing meets up again at Fallon for a fully blown STRIKE det that lasts three weeks. Here, all the units integrate what they have learnt independently of each other into all-encompassing air wing tactics that would be employed in the event of war.

'This brings us up to where we are now – at the start of our second at-sea period. While aboard, we will undertake a CompTuEx, which is essentially a series of smaller exercises that go to make up one big exercise. These are tailored so as to provide intermediate training not only for the air wing, but for the ship's crew as well, for as with squadron personnel, many of the sailors aboard CV 64 will also be first time taxy directors, catapult officers and air traffic controllers, to name but three trades that go to make up the vessel's huge complement.

The air wing of the late 1990s has the F/A-18C firmly at its heart, and with CVW-2 touted as the model force structure for carrier aviation into the twenty-first century, it comes as no surprise to find thirty-six Lot XV Hornets crowding the deck of CV 64 when the vessel is at sea. Chained down between bow cat two and waist cat three, these four jets have a total airframe value of $160 million when devoid of external stores. Competition exists between the three light strike units embarked on 'Connie' in respect to mission proficiency and flying skill 'around the boat', but as Lt Hal 'Bull' Schmitt of VFA-137 explained, everyone is aware of what the ultimate goal of the air wing is: 'Although there is a healthy rivalry maintained between the units, when it comes down to it these guys in our sister squadrons could be potentially saving your life in a real-world combat situation by doing the air-to-air stuff while you're dropping bombs. We are therefore fully appreciative of the fact that we are all on the same side.'

When compared with its single-engined predecessor, the A-7 Corsair II, the Hornet is a dream to handle on the approach to a carrier, its ultra-responsive GE F404-GE-402 EPE (Enhanced Performance Engine) permitting the pilot to extricate himself from any potentially watery 'hole' he may have dug himself rapidly into when lining up to land. This abundance of near instantaneous thrust has combined with the generous flying surface area (leading edge slats and trailing edge drooping ailerons) to bestow upon the Hornet recovery characteristics that have made it one of the safest aircraft ever to be sent to sea with the Navy. 'Snake 212' (BuNo 164734) glides over the roundown looking good for an 'OK Three' pass landing.

'Called an Intermediate Training Assessment [ITA], this phase is scrutinised by AIRPAC [Air Forces Pacific] from every possible angle. From a squadron point of view, our success at operating in "blue water" conditions with no divert field capability is assessed. Missions flown in conjunction with the ITA include semi-advanced attacks on inland targets in the southern California region utilising AWACS, EW and fighter support in the prosecution of these limited Alpha strikes – the S-3B and SH-60F units will prove their respective skills by exercising with surface and sub-surface threats.

'Having completed the ITA, we will return ashore for a number of weeks to further hone our specific mission taskings in light of the examiners' findings, before embarking on the carrier once again early in the New Year for our final Advanced Training Assessments [typically a ten- followed by a fourteen-day at-sea period] and graduation, which is essentially "a check in the block" from AIRPAC stating that we are all trained up and ready to deploy on cruise.'

As this book went to print, Cdr Philman, Lt Seth and Lt(jg) Schmitt – plus the remaining complement of CV 64's battle group – were putting into effect on a daily basis what they had learned off the coast of California, and over the Nevada desert, in the potentially hostile environment of the Persian Gulf.

A 'B-B stacker' from VMFA-323 takes a breather after having just helped to uplift this inert (hence its blue colouring) Mk 82R retarded fin bomb on to the outer starboard wing pylon. The steel rods at either end of the weapon are attached by the 'ordies' so as to give them more purchase when manually attaching bombs to aircraft. Both these Mk 82Rs were expended over CVW-2's island bombing range during the air wing's work-up phase.

'Snake 212' is carefully positioned alongside elevator one without the help of a tractor after completing its bombing mission. Swarming around the jet are armourers, deck handlers, a solitary 'chock and chain' man, and one of the ship's fire crews. Once safely shackled to the deck, VMFA-323's dedicated groundcrew will refuel and rearm the Hornet so as to have it ready for the next launch period, scheduled to commence some seventy-five minutes after the landing cycle has been completed. Cdr Dave 'Deke' Philman, CO of VFA-151: 'The hot turnaround of the F/A-18 is directly attributable to the new technology embodied in the jet's systems. In the old days, we would invariably return to the ship in the A-7 after completing a mission with niggling avionics snags or hydraulic leaks that would need repairing before the jet could fly its next sortie. This duly resulted in longer cycles of one hour and forty-five minutes. With the Hornet, and newer Tomcats, you usually only have to top up the fuel and upload new ordnance, thus cutting cycle times down by half an hour. The swiftness of the F/A-18 turnaround is perhaps best illustrated by the fact that the new pilot arriving to pre-flight the returned jet can't touch certain areas of the airframe during his deck-level walkround because they are still hot from the previous sortie!'

Embarked Aircraft

VF-2 'Bounty Hunters' – F-14D Tomcat
163895/100   159630/101   164602/102   164350/103
161163/104   164603/105   163897/106   163903/107
163898/110   159613/111   159619/112   159628/114
159600/115

VMFA-323 'Death Rattlers' – F/A-18C Hornet
164721/200   164722/201   164725/203   164727/204
164875/205   164730/206   164731/207   164733/211
164734/212   164696/214

VFA-151 'Vigilantes' – F/A-18C Hornet
164703/300   164739/301   164897/302   164700/303
164708/304   164710/305   164713/306   164716/307
164719/310   164737/311   164740/312   164896/313

VFA-137 'Kestrels' – F/A-18C Hornet
164712/400   164698/401   164701/402   164704/403
164709/404   164693/405   164715/406   164718/407
164720/410   164707/411   164736/412   164895/413

VAW-116 'Sun Kings' – E-2C Group II Hawkeye
164112/600   164484/601   164487/602   164488/603

HS-2 'Golden Falcons' – SH-60F/HH-60H Seahawk
SH-60F
164447/610   164456/611   164088/612   163288/615
164084/616

HH-60H
165118/613   165117/614

VAQ-131 'Lancers' – EA-6B Prowler
163525/620   164402/621   163524/622   164401/623

VS-38 'Red Griffins' – S-3B Viking
160573/700   160596/701   160572/702   160126/703
160567/704   159409/705   160124/706   159731/707

VQ-5 'Sea Shadows' 'Det Charlie' – ES-3A Viking
159420/721

Each toting a live Mk 83 LDGB (Low-Drag General purpose Bomb) on their outer wing pylons, five F/A-18Cs sit idling along 'Four Row' in anticipation of the next launch cycle. The jets are also equipped with AIM-9L acquisition rounds, which will allow them to practise ACM both before and after they have delivered their ordnance on the island target off the Californian coast. The range used during this phase of the CompTuEx was deemed to be a co-usage target due to its employment by the entire air wing. New pilots to CVW-2 were initially tasked with simply flying to the target and familiarising themselves with its layout, topography and simulated SAM and EW threats. Once adjudged to be comfortable with the island's geography, the JOs were unleashed on the range in bombed-up aircraft identically configured to the Hornets depicted here. On a typical cycle during the exercise six F/A-18Cs (two from each unit), two F-14Ds and single examples of the E-2C, EA-6B and S-3B would launch as an integrated strike package, capable of generating both offensive and defensive mission profiles in the same sortie.

Above:
The pilot of 'Switch 303' (BuNo 164700) gingerly taxies his jet forward under the guidance of the plane director, who is standing off to the left of bow cat one. In the foreground in front of the 'yellow-shirt' is the cat shuttle itself, retracting back down the track following the previous launch. While the hook up men prepare to go to work on the jet's hold-back device, two troubleshooting aircraft checkers (hence their customised 'float coats') from VFA-151 start their visual scrutiny of the Hornet at its radome, and quickly work aft – they should have finished their inspection by the time the hook up crew signal that the F/A-18C has been attached to the shuttle.

'Switch 312' (BuNo 164740) is firmly 'in the groove' for an 'OK Three' pass in the notebook of VFA-151's LSO. The jet's rugged undercarriage is built by McDonnell Douglas contractor Cleveland Pneumatic, and is stressed to cope with a descent rate of up to twenty-four feet per second, a figure rarely reached in anything but the worst sea conditions. Like the remaining two Hornet units in CVW-2, the 'Vigilantes' are the original owners of these Lot XV aircraft, a factor greatly appreciated by the unit's CO: 'We've had them for about three-and-a-half years, and it is the first time in my career that I've got to fly jets this new. It means that our maintainers know exactly how these aircraft have been serviced, and by whom. This effectively means that the pilots don't have to worry about being assigned a weary jet from the so-called lemon lot!'

Left:
Streaming wingtip vortices as it passes over the deck following a wave off during its approach to land, 'Switch 312' accelerates away back into the carrier's 800ft circuit. An aircraft is usually waved off when the preceding machine has failed to clear the 'wires' quickly enough, or the latter have not had time to return into position across the deck. With aircraft scheduled to land back on board every forty-five seconds during a recovery cycle, and fuel states getting critical at the end of a sortie, the LSOs and arrestor crew have to work in unison to ensure that there are not too many wave offs in a typical landing period.

Things can get a little noisy up on the bow of the ship when the recovering jets are marshalled forward to make way for the rest of the cycle, thereby joining the aircraft sitting at idle awaiting unshackling for the next launch phase. Surrounded by 'ordies', the pilot of 'Switch 303' raises his hands in the cockpit so the deckcrewmen can visibly see that they are safely away from the weapons activation panel. Once assured of

this, a team of armourers will rush in and insert the red tagged safety pins in the pylon firing mechanisms and Sidewinder rails, thus rendering them inert. Unlike many other Hornet units in today's light strike community, VFA-151 have more of a fighter than attack background, having previously flown both F-3B Demons and F-4 Phantom IIs. Indeed, while equipped with the latter jet the 'Vigilantes' completed seven combat

tours to Vietnam, downing a single MiG-17 during its time in action. Forward deployed with CVW-5 at NAF Atsugi, Japan, in 1973, the unit changed its designation to VFA-151 in 1986 when it traded its F-4Ss for F/A-18As. It finally returned to CONUS in 1991 following the retirement of its long-term 'home', USS *Midway* (CV-41), and after re-equipping with Lot XV F/A-18Cs in 1993, was assigned to CVW-2.

Bombs dropped on the island range, 'Falcon 401' (BuNo 164698) strains at the 'wire' as the pilot keeps the throttle wide open until the jet has stopped. Note the fully extended trailing edge drooping ailerons, tailplanes set to maximum deflection, and toed-in rudders. The last of four units specially formed to operate the first F/A-18As issued to the light strike community on the east coast, VFA-137 was commissioned on 1 July 1985 at NAS Cecil Field, Florida. After participating in several Atlantic cruises with CVW-13 on board USS *Coral Sea* (CV-43), the 'Kestrels' were reassigned to CVW-6 on board USS *Forrestal* (CV-59) when its former home was retired in 1989. This fate also befell its 'new' carrier some two years later, and with the subsequent disbanding of its controlling air wing, VFA-137 was transferred to the west coast, and the newly reorganised CVW-2, in 1993.

Above:
Just a lick of afterburner is visible as 'Falcon 401' departs waist cat four at 150-plus knots. Lt Hal 'Bull' Schmitt, VFA-137: 'The use of afterburner on launch is dictated by the weight of the aircraft. In some configurations the afterburner will be engaged before the catapult launches, but in others you push the throttles up as the stroke is fired. The catapult on a nuclear ship is configured to give a steadily increasing acceleration during the stroke, but on a conventional ship like this one it all comes on with a bang – it's a pretty good shot!'

Opposite:
The refuelling boom fitted at the base of the EA-6B's windscreen is canted to the right in order to reduce its level of obstruction to the pilot, particularly when the latter is lining up to land. The small excrescence at the base of the boom houses a receiver for the jet's AN/ALQ-126 DECM (Deceptive Electronic Counter-Measures) suite – a second receiver is sited at the rear of the fin-top 'football'.

A fully-tinted visor comes in very useful when taxiing into the sun on a crowded, moving, deck as the pilot of 'Skybolt 623' finds out as he steers his jet towards the stern of CV 64. The AN/ALQ-99F Tactical Jamming System (TJS) pods fitted to the jet combine with the AGM-88 missile to give the crew the flexibility to prosecute both 'soft' and 'hard' targets, the former possessing two jamming transmitters that can obliterate all known emitter frequency bands. The ram air turbine built into the nose of the pod generates electrical power for the unit once the aircraft is airborne. The pods are designed to operate over specific frequencies, and these cannot be altered once the aircraft has launched from the carrier – hence Prowlers typically operate with three pods fitted, all of which are set to cover different frequency bands.

Preflighting an aircraft as large and as complex as a Prowler is a long and involved affair, so the workload is duly shared between its four-man crew. Having completed the deck-level checks, the pilot and two of his ECMOs (Electronic Counter-Measures Officers) stow their gear prior to climbing into 'Skybolt 623' (164401). This particular jet was the 168th out of 170 EA-6Bs built for the Navy, being delivered to the fleet by Grumman in 1992. Like the remaining three aircraft in VAQ-131, the aircraft boasts full Block 89 upgrades, making it the most up-to-date EW platform in the world. Similar to the equipment fitted to the preceding Block 86 jets, but with the addition of a halon fire extinguisher system, these aircraft are equipped with SSA-4.0 software for the ALQ-99 suite, which enables them to make better use of their principal offensive weapon, the AGM-88 HARM. An improved Tactical EA-6B Mission Support system (TEAMS) was also issued to the unit with the upgrading of its jets, thus allowing VAQ-131 to work up a greater range of strike profiles prior to launching with other members of CVW-2.

Nicknamed the 'beer can', the rear-hemisphere AN/ALQ-126 receiver is clearly visible in this shot of 'Skybolt 622' (BuNo 163524) taxying aft in preparation for launch from waist cat four. Built as a Block 86 machine and delivered to VAQ-131 directly from the manufacturer in late 1989, this particular jet served as 'Skybolt 605' during *Desert Storm*, flying from the deck of the now retired *Ranger* as part of Battle Force *Zulu*. CV 61 fulfilled the demanding role of 'night carrier' for the latter force during the conflict.

The plane director keeps his arms raised to signal to the crew of 'Skybolt 622' that the jet's wings are in the process of unfolding into the extended position. Once down, the wing will be visually examined by the squadron's safety crewmen to ensure that the hinging mechanisms have locked properly. Having checked the hinges, they will then signal in the affirmative to the plane director, who will in turn lower his arms, and thus visually confirm that the aircraft is ready to launch. This jet appears to have acquired a replacement radome from an anonymous donor back at its NAS Whidbey Island, Washington, home prior to deploying on board 'Connie'.

A trio of ECMOs await the signal to climb aboard their jet, spotted over the stern of CV 64. During the CompTuEx most units within CVW-2 were operating 'hot' turnarounds that would see the same aircraft (two Prowlers in VAQ-131's case) used throughout the day, bar any technical snags. This essentially meant that while one jet was aloft, the recently returned aircraft would be serviced and preflighted in time to launch on the next cycle. By operating in this fashion the air wing becomes exposed to the true sortie tempo achieved on *WestPac*, where most aircrew complete two missions a day.

Below:
Safely chocked and shackled at the end of yet another training sortie, 'Skybolt 623' is refuelled in preparation for its next launch in just over an hour. The aircrew can be seen still in the throes of extricating themselves from the jet – not a procedure to be taken lightly in view of the fact that the cockpit sits a good ten feet off the deck. The rear fuselage-mounted 'birdcage' avionics bay ('extensible equipment platform' in official Navy parlance) has been hinged open on this jet to allow new LOX (Liquid Oxygen) bottles to be fitted by squadron technicians – these are crucial in keeping cool the myriad electronics fitted inside the jet. Other equipment mounted in the locale includes power supply boxes (for various EW systems like the AN/ALQ-41 signal tracking breaker), the ARC-105 radio receiver/transmitter, the AN/APN-153 Doppler navigation system and the gyroscope assembly.

Hawkeye squadrons have kept their traditional high visibility markings into the 1990s by dint of their AEW role, which should keep them well away from the prying eyes of the enemy; a personal escort of Tomcats and Hornets should also deter all but the most determined of adversaries. VAW-116's aircraft were exceptionally colourful even for an E-2 squadron, their CO insisting that they adopt a new motif in place of the traditional sunburst and axe emblem (see chapter one). A squadron-wide competition was held in early 1996, and the winning entry was duly applied to all four Hawkeyes, as seen here – note the slight differences between the hand-painted artwork.

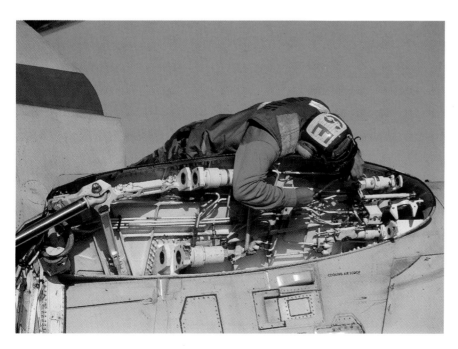

The complex wing folding mechanism on a VAW-116 E-2C is checked over by a prone technician between sorties. The exposed nature of the wing fold is both a blessing and a bugbear to maintenance crews, for although its construction affords the latter easy access to the screw jacks, actuators and hydraulic lines that physically move the outer wing, this openness provides no protection from the corrosive elements encountered on a windswept deck.

The Hawkeye is both the largest and most expensive aircraft within any air wing, and therefore extra diligence is required when marshalling the aircraft around the deck between sorties. As mentioned earlier, the E-2 is also the first aircraft launched at the start of a cycle, thus dictating its traditional parking spot beneath the island from where it can reach the bow cats with little fuss.

Most major maintenance tasks can be completed on the hangar deck away from the elements, but the changing of a Hamilton Standard reverse pitch constant-speed propeller is a job that requires the use of specialist lifting equipment too tall for erection anywhere else but on the flightdeck. The alignment of the prop to the gearbox mechanism is a task that requires great precision – no easy matter on a greasy deck which is constantly pitching up and down as the carrier slices through the water at twenty-plus knots.

Above:
Vortices stream away from composite propeller blades as 'Sun King 603' is banked to starboard immediately after completing its cat stroke. The two-man flightcrew on board the aircraft usually share the high workload associated with the take-off, the pilot being responsible for physically flying the aircraft after launch while the co-pilot cycles away the undercarriage and the long-span ailerons and Fowler flaps.

The Hawkeye is considered to be one of the more challenging aircraft to land back on board ship, thanks to the torque generated by the aircraft's propellers. Although the turboprop engines are more responsive to power changes than their jet equivalents, alterations in throttle settings can adversely affect the E-2 in both the vertical and horizontal plane. If not properly countered, this can have dire consequences for a machine that boasts an 80ft 7in wingspan, greater than any other aircraft in the air wing. In effect, this means the pilot only enjoys a ten-foot lateral variance margin on approach. On the positive side, the landing speed for the Hawkeye is considerably less than that associated with its jet-powered counterparts – crews aim to recover at 100 knots indicated airspeed, thirty knots of which is provided by the ship, reducing the effective landing speed to just seventy knots.

The hook-up man uses a hand-held torch to check that the launch bar on 'Sun King 603' (BuNo 164488) has successfully engaged the catapult shuttle. Although the prospect of being sucked into a jet intake mortifies deck crewmen, the whirling blades of the E-2 command even greater respect. Forward-facing receivers for the Litton AN/ALR-73 Passive Defense System (PDS) are housed immediately behind the protective black oval painted on the aircraft's nose, these being able to detect hostile electro-magnetic emitters at up to twice the range of the aircraft's radar suite. Further antennae are fitted at the extreme rear of the E-2's fuselage and on its outer fins.

Looking at the overall 'greyscape' presented by the aircraft ranged in front of CV 64's island, it is hard to believe that for many decades US Navy jets were among the most colourfully marked combat machines in the world. From this elevated viewpoint the 'shoulder-mounted' ALD-9 low band phase measuring direction finding system fitted to VQ-5 'Det Charlie's' ES-3A is clearly visible beneath its folded wings.

'Shadow 721' (BuNo 159420) was the sole ES-3A aboard 'Connie' during the October/November work-up, the sheer rarity of the type preventing 'Det Charlie' from embarking with a typical frontline strength of two jets – only sixteen ES-3As were converted by Lockheed in the early 1990s. As the controlling unit of all ES-3As on the west coast, VQ-5 won the coveted Arleigh Burke Trophy for the Pacific Fleet as a result of its battle efficiency in 1995.

The crew of 'Griffin 701' (BuNo 160596) lower the jet's outer wings in preparation for launch from bow cat one. The aircraft is kitted out in the near standard dual role configuration that has become familiar within the S-3 community since the demise of the KA-6D – an Aero ID 300 US gal fuel tank on the port wing pylon and a Douglas D-704 buddy buddy hose-and-drogue refuelling pod to starboard. This particular aircraft was the youngest of the eight S-3Bs assigned to VS-38 in 1996, being the 175th (out of a total of 187) Viking built by Lockheed. It was delivered to the Navy in 1977.

A catapult officer inserts a purple-coloured metal hold-back into the removable hold-back bar that will be attached to the rear of the Viking's nose gear once it has engaged the launch shuttle. This device effectively restrains the aircraft until the hourglass-shaped metal hold-back (replacements are seen stored at the crewman's feet) breaks when the predetermined load exerted on it by the combined force of the catapult and the aircraft's engines can no longer be withstood – this force is calculated to be sufficient to enable the aircraft to launch successfully. Each hold-back is colour-coded and precision-machined for the specific launch criterion of the individual aircraft types within the air wing. The F/A-18 and the F-14 use a 'repeatable release' hydraulic hold-back device in place of the one-shot frangible hold-backs.

The Viking's twin TF34-GE-400 turbofan engines were specially designed for the Lockheed ASW jet, giving the aircraft both 'dash speed' potential when transiting to its operational area and sufficient economy when throttled back to endow the S-3 with an unrivalled loiter time on station. The engines also possess a low stalling speed, thus making the Viking one of the easier aircraft to fly back aboard ship. Note the open APU exhaust vent directly below the Sensor Operator's (SENSO) window on 'Griffin 705' (BuNo 159409, which was the oldest S-3B in VS-38, having initially been delivered to the Navy in mid-1974).

Having been waved off on its approach to land, VS-38's CAG jet (BuNo 160573) accelerates away with its tailhook, undercarriage and trailing edge flaps extended. The main landing gear (a strengthened version of that fitted to the classic F-8 Crusader), wings, tail and engine pods on the S-3 were designed and built by sub-contractors Vought. This veteran Viking also served as 'Griffin 700' during the unit's *WestPac* in 1995.

Although principally tasked with providing inner-zone ASW protection for CV 64 and her battle group, HS-2 also conducts combat SAR and vertrep missions with its HH-60H Seahawks. Illustrating their ability to perform the latter role, the 'Golden Falcons' sortied both their utility helicopters ('Hunters 613' and '614' – BuNos 165118 and 165117) for an hour-long vertrep with the Henry J Kaiser class oiler USNS *Rappahannock* (T-AO 204). The latter vessel was actually conducting an unrep (underway replenishment) with 'Connie' throughout the vertrep, topping up the carrier's stocks of fuel oil and JP-5. All foodstuffs, spare parts and mail had to be boxed up and transferred in pallets slung beneath the HH-60s during the rendezvous with the oiler.

Above:
The first crewman keeps a watchful eye on the deck as his pilot gently winds on the power and climbs away from the recently delivered pallet – both men are in constant voice communication with each other throughout the flight. The empty strop hook can be seen immediately below the crewman, its strong 'jaws' silhouetted against the external tank by the low morning sun. The HH-60H can carry underslung loads weighing up to 8,000lb.

The pilot prepares to open the hook 'jaws' on the command of the first crewman, seen here peering deckward at the pallet. Once the helicopter has left the immediate area, a team of forklift-driving deckcrew will rush over and retrieve the pallets in order to make room for the next drop. The rubberised strops used to attach the load to the helicopter will be bundled together and affixed to an 'empty' HH-60 to be returned to the oiler.

The two HH-60Hs on board CV 64 were the newest aircraft within CVW-2, having only been delivered to HS-2 from the Sikorsky plant in late 1995. Their age contrasts markedly with the US Navy's primary vertrep platform, the venerable CH-46D Sea Knight of pre-Vietnam War vintage. The Navy recently announced its Helicopter Master Plan, which they hope will see some 134 CH-60s (a derivative of the US Army's UH-60L Black Hawk) procured to replace the CH-46D, HH-60H and H-3 helicopters in the utility role. The 'new' helicopter will combine the navalised Seahawk's folding tail cone and automatic flight control system with the 'off-the-shelf' fuselage and mechanicals of the standard UH-60, thus producing a significant saving in development costs for the Navy. The plan also states that all 273 Seahawks presently in frontline service will be remanufactured to a universal SH-60R standard, thus doing away with ASW or utility-only helicopters within carrier-based helicopter squadrons.

Above:
Although superficially similar in appearance to Sikorsky's UTTAS (Utility Tactical Transport Aircraft System) winning S-70/UH-60 Black Hawk, the Seahawk embodies a number of significant modifications that have allowed it to perform effectively at sea. These include a more robust transmission; electric power folding and braking for the main rotor; a dual wheel gear located beneath the rear fuselage in place of the UH-60's tail wheel; simplified main gear, fitted with multi-disc brakes; extensive anti-corrosive finish; incorporation of the RAST (Recovery Assist, Secure and Traverse) landing system; greater fuel capacity and the installation of a hover-in-flight refuelling system (HIFRS); advanced automatic flight control system (AFCS); elimination of the port sliding door and fitment of a down-sized starboard door; installation of ASW mission equipment, sensor station and twenty-five-tube sonobuoy rack; an optional rescue hoist; an uprated environmental control system; emergency flotation equipment; and a folding tailplane. This HH-60H is being marshalled back to its allotted parking spot, having recently completed a three-hour plane-guard sortie.

Right:
'Launch the COD!' If a visiting C-2 is scheduled to depart during a launch cycle it is usually the first aircraft catapulted off the ship. During a *WestPac* VRC-30 will fly far and wide in support of the deployed carrier, staging through shore bases like Diego Garcia, Bahrain and Perth in order to shuttle mail, vital stores and personnel, flown in directly from the US on board dedicated USAF and Navy transport aircraft, to the awaiting CV/CVN.

Left:
Undoubtedly the ugliest aircraft to operate regularly from the deck of a CV/CVN, the humble C-2A is nevertheless the most keenly awaited arrival by the 5,000-strong crew when it appears in the landing pattern overhead the carrier. Why? Because its capacious hold is usually stuffed with mail bags full of letters from 'the folks back home'. On this particular day the Greyhound (from VRC-30) had flown in from NAS North Island with a consignment of VIPs rather than mail. Utilising the same 80ft 7in wing as that fitted to its sleeker Northrop-Grumman AEW cousin, the C-2 has to be precisely aligned with the centreline of the deck on approach to land.

Above:
Instructional 'graffiti' is emblazoned all over the lower surface of the C-2's fuselage. Up to thirty-nine passengers or 18,000lb of palletised cargo can be carried by the Greyhound at speeds approaching 310 knots. VRC-30 'Providers' is the west coast COD (Carrier On-Board Delivery) unit, flying some fifteen-plus aircraft from its base at NAS North Island.

Steaming near to her maximum speed of thirty knots, CV 64 prepares to welcome an EA-6B back on board. Meanwhile, forward of the island a recently returned F-14D is surrounded by armourers as the jet's external pylons are rendered safe once again. The 80,000-ton *Constellation* relies on General Electric high and low pressure steam turbines (eight in total) to generate the 280,000 shaft horsepower required for it to attain launch and recovery speeds. The high pressure turbines were all replaced during the SLEP, while the low pressure machinery was taken out and thoroughly overhauled.

This spread and overleaf:
Constellation is seen at speed off the coast of southern California between launch and recovery cycles from the vantage point of the HS-2 HH-60H plane guard. Thanks to her recent SLEP, 'Connie' is likely to be the last conventionally powered CV retired from frontline service – this will probably occur sometime around 2008. The prominent mast

fitted to the starboard catwalk behind the F/A-18s is known as the *Kennedy* or *Belknap* pole, and was retrofitted to CV 64 (and all other US carriers) in the aftermath of the terrible collision at night between these two vessels in the Mediterranean in November 1975. Navigation lights are mounted on the pole so as to allow supporting vessels to determine the carrier's heading at night. The

ship's primary navigation light is fitted atop the masthead on the island's main mast, and an accurate fix on the carrier can be deduced by comparing the relative positions of the two lights. A wind speed and direction indicator is also affixed to the top of the catwalk pole.

Westlant 90

Date: May 1990
Location: mid-Atlantic
Aircraft Carrier: HMS *Ark Royal* (RO 7)

With its flightdeck secured following the recovery of its air wing, a thoroughly drenched HMS *Ark Royal* sails on towards North America while the recently returned aircraft are marshalled back to their allotted tie-down areas – for the Sea Harrier FRS 1s of No 801 Sqn that means the fantail of the ship. The stern of a carrier has traditionally been 'fighter country' in most navies for a number of decades, and the Royal Navy is no exception. Pushing the 20,000lb plus aircraft back aft is a five-ton deck tractor, which relies on a low-geared diesel engine similar in design to that found in a Routemaster bus to provide ample motive power, even on the most slippery of decks.

Prior to its full-time commitment to policing the eastern Mediterranean as part of Operation *Deny Flight* during the civil war in the former Yugoslavia, the Royal Navy would regularly send a carrier task force across the Atlantic for a concentrated period of exercises with elements of the US Navy and Air Force and the Canadian Armed Forces. Lasting two to three months, this deployment was known as a *Westlant*.

In 1990 HMS *Invincible* (RO 5) had seen in the New Year while on *Westlant 89*, the carrier finally returning to British waters in mid-February. Two months later, sister-ship HMS *Ark Royal* (RO 7) pulled out of Portsmouth and embarked its air wing, prior to heading for the warm climes of the Mediterranean for several weeks of exercising with other NATO navies. This work-up was part of the vessel's preparation for its impending foray across the Atlantic on *Westlant 90*, and by the time the carrier steered a course for the Azores in late April, its air wing was operating at peak performance. A total of nineteen fixed-and rotary-wing aircraft crowded the carrier's deck during the deployment, this figure comprising eight Sea Harrier FRS 1s of No 801 Sqn, six Sea King HAS 6s and a solitary HAS 5 of No 820 Sqn, three Sea King AEW 2As of No 849 Sqn's 'B' Flight, and a single Sea King HC 4 of No 846 Sqn – today, an *Invincible* class carrier will rarely deploy with more than fifteen aircraft embarked.

Once in the open waters of the Atlantic, *Ark Royal* was joined by a variety of escorts and support ships including the Batch 2 Type 42 destroyer HMS *Glasgow* (D 88), the Type 22 frigates HMSs *Cumberland* (F 85) and *Brave* (F 94), and the RFAs *Olna* (A 123) and *Fort Grange* (A 385). These vessels would provide the air wing with a variety of opportunities to hone their respective skills in anticipation of some rigorous exercising with their American and Canadian allies. For example, No 849 Sqn quickly deployed two of its Sea King AEW 2As to the fleet oiler *Olna* for several days in order to both relieve the congestion on the cramped deck space of its parent carrier, and to gain valuable experience in operating away from its spares supply and sophisticated mission briefing infrastructure. During its stay, the 'B' Flight det was commanded by a senior lieutenant, who was charged with generating and planning the two five-hour sorties that were flown each day, briefing Commander (AIR) back on *Ark* as to the availability of the AEW assets in respect to the operations of the Sea Harriers, and overseeing any maintenance work required to keep the two helicopters airworthy.

With a full complement of eight Sea Harriers at its disposal, No 801 Sqn kept busy generating fighter, reconnaissance and strike

Safely 'chocked and chained', FRS 1 ZE698 has the steerable tow bar used to position it into its allotted spot removed from its nosewheel shackle. The colour of a sailor's surcoat denotes his (or her) job whilst operating out on the deck: brown is worn by airframe and engine technicians, blue indicates an aircraft handler and yellow flightdeck directors. ZE698 was the last FRS 1 built for the FAA, being delivered to No 801 Sqn in February 1990 after spending some sixteen months in storage at RAF St Athan, in Wales. In February 1995 it created history firstly by flying the last operational sortie for the FRS 1 in FAA service (a Combat Air Support mission over Bosnia), followed soon after by the final launch of a frontline FRS 1 from a fleet carrier – it achieved both while with No 800 Sqn on board *Invincible*. ZE698 has now been converted to FA 2 configuration.

sorties which would invariably involve one or more of the escort vessels acting both as 'targets' and fighter controllers, depending on the mission tasking. Towed 'splash targets' were also utilised for both gunnery and live ordnance runs, the sledge-like device (which measured about six feet square and was made of timber) being deployed behind the carrier at the end of a 600ft wire. Constructed with various cross-members between its side boards, which not only allowed it to float but also generated a plume of spray that was easily spotted by an attacking pilot, the target was ideal for rocket, gunnery and practice bomb training. The line of attack adopted by the pilot running in to hit the sledge was from a 45° angle on the port bow of the carrier, which made it easier for observers on *Ark* to monitor the jet's angle of dive.

All firing aircraft were controlled by Commander (AIR), ensconced in Flyco (the flying bridge) aboard the carrier – he was also responsible for making sure that the area surrounding the target was clear, and that each of the Sea Harrier pilots fired off his ordnance safely. Fall of shot was accurately measured in angular terms by squadron personnel observing from both the carrier and from a trailing frigate, or helicopter, positioned aft of the beam at 90° to the target itself. Simulated Sea Eagle firings were also carried out against *Glasgow* and *Cumberland* during the transatlantic crossing, as well as air combat exercises, which pitted single aircraft against multiple targets, and high level intercepts where the jets were

Having refuelled the SHARs tanks with Avtur and replenished the water injection system with demineralised distillate, surcoated deck crewmen wait patiently as the carrier is steered into wind in preparation for launching its aircraft. The blurred horizon behind FRS 1 XZ457 denotes that its pilot has already strapped in and 'spooled up' his mount's Rolls-Royce Pegasus Mk 104 engine. This particular jet is arguably the most famous Sea Harrier ever built, downing four Argentine aircraft (two A-4Q Skyhawks and two Daggers, a score unmatched by any other FRS 1) while in action with No 800 Sqn aboard HMS *Hermes* in May/June 1982. It also dropped three 1,000lb bombs on Goose Green and expended 680 rounds of 30mm cannon shell during the course of sixty-six operational sorties. Having seen almost thirteen years of near constant frontline flying with both fleet-serving fighter units, XZ457 was sent to British Aerospace for conversion to FA 2 specification in late 1993, before being reissued to No 899 Sqn in March 1994. It subsequently suffered a serious engine fire while in flight near Yeovilton on 20 October 1995, and although the pilot managed to return the jet safely to base, it has yet to be rebuilt.

Below:
The tie-down chains take the strain as *Ark* heels into wind in order to achieve its Designated Flying Course (DFC) at the start of another cycle of ops. This FRS 1 (ZA193) boasts a Carrier Bomb/Light Store (CBLS) on the centreline rack between the twin Aden cannon pods and a finless AIM-9L Sidewinder acquisition round on its single port missile rail. Both stores were heavily employed during squadron work-ups in preparation for joint exercises with US and Canadian forces during *Westlant 90*. ZA193 flew some sixty-one sorties with No 800 Sqn during the Falklands War, being involved in the first bombing strike on Port Stanley airfield on 1 May 1982 and later downing one of three Daggers destroyed on the 24th of that month. After a decade of flying both with the FAA and the Aerospace & Armaments Experimental Establishment (A&AEE), ZA193 was lost off Cyprus on 28 May 1992 when its pilot – No 800 Sqn's Lt Pete 'Whizzer' Wilson – was forced to eject following the failure of the forward pitch nozzle during an approach to landing on *Invincible*.

vectored onto 'bogies' by either No 849 Sqn or ship-based fighter controllers.

No 801 Sqn was commanded during *Westlant 90* by Falklands War veteran Lt-Cdr M W 'Soapy' Watson, who had been the junior pilot with this same unit exactly eight years earlier (due to a chronic shortage of Sea Harrier-qualified senior pilots in the early 1990s, this tour of duty was in fact Watson's second back-to-back posting in a command position, for he had served as boss of No 800 Sqn between January 1988 and January 1990). An ex-Sea King 'driver' prior to his transition to Sea Harriers in late 1981, 'Soapy' had completed innumerable sorties while in the South Atlantic.

The Operation *Corporate* connection within the unit at the time also stretched to its Senior Pilot (or SPLOT), Lt-Cdr D H S Dave Morgan DSC, who had been the RAF exchange officer instructing with No 899 Sqn at the time of the Falklands crisis. During the course of the war Morgan had downed two helicopters and two Skyhawks while flying with No 800 Sqn from HMS *Hermes* (R 12) – a score unequalled by any of his contemporaries. Upon his return to Britain, he resigned his commission in the RAF and transferred to the Fleet Air Arm. Other pilots of note within the squadron in 1990

Above left:
Lt Paul Simmonds-Short (also a successful FRS 1 'ejectee', having 'banged out' of ZA191 in October 1989 after clipping the radar mast of *Ark Royal* during a squadron flypast) has completed the transition from horizontal to vertical flight and is lined up alongside spot six for landing, all the while monitoring the actions of the Flight Deck Officer (FDO) aboard the carrier. All 21,500lb of thrust generated by the jet's Pegasus engine is required at this stage in the flight to keep the Sea Harrier aloft, as any aerodynamic assistance offered by the wing has long since evaporated with the pilot selecting nozzles down for landing. Once in the correct position off the port side of the carrier, the pilot will carefully manoeuvre over the deck and then reduce power to land, briefly 'blipping' the throttle just feet away from touchdown in order to arrest the jet's sink rate and cushion his arrival back aboard. Like ZA193, this jet (XZ459) also participated in Operation *Corporate* with No 800 Sqn and took part in the 'May Day' raid on Port Stanley airfield – it flew fifty-three sorties during the conflict and shared in the destruction of the freighter *Rio Carcarana*. The aircraft has since been upgraded to FA 2 specs.

Once back on board, the pilot is quickly directed forward to make room for the next recovery, which will occur just thirty seconds later. A typical four-ship flight of SHARs is usually recovered within a minute-and-a-half.

were Lts A R 'Mum' Davis and Dale Omeara, both of whom had previously served with the Royal Australian Navy's Fleet Air Arm prior to moving permanently to the RN in 1983/4. They had been part of the great exodus of fixed-wing pilots who had found themselves suddenly grounded, or facing careers in the Royal Australian Air Force, when the mooted purchase of *Invincible* as a replacement for the weary HMAS *Melbourne* (A 21) fell through as a result of the Falklands War.

Typically, the largest contingent of aircrew to be found on a British carrier in the 1990s hails from the embarked ASW unit, and on *Westlant 90* that meant the 'flying fish' of No 820 Sqn. Far from being just another deployment for this veteran outfit, the unit was actually debuting the new Sea King HAS 6 in 'blue water' service. Of the seven 'cabs' embarked in *Ark*, five of them had been converted to

Nothing moves on the deck without the permission (or guidance) of the FDO. Here, he holds a SHAR idling prior to launch while the pilot completes his final checks on engine power and control freedoms. The FDO will also quickly perform a series of external checks on the jet to ensure that the stores pylons have been rendered live by the activation of the Master Armament Safety Switch (MASS), and that the red ejection seat pins, which signify that the pilot has indeed activated his Martin-Baker seat, are stored in the cockpit coaming rack.

A red surcoat with a black stripe down the middle labels its wearer as a 'bombhead', tasked with loading all types of weaponry and external stores onto the aircraft's four wing pylons and single centreline station. In addition to the huge Sea Eagle missile, arguably the heaviest weapon regularly up-loaded beneath the SHAR's modest flying surface is the 1,000lb Mk 13 Heavy Explosive (HE) bomb, which usually requires a team of five Air Weapons specialists to see it safely attached to the pylon, even with the use of two lifting hoists.

Once the live bomb is secured onto the pylon, the armourers torque-load the weapon to the release unit to ensure that it will not move around in flight. The correct loading of a bomb of this size onto the outer pylons of a Sea Harrier is crucial, because if it 'hangs up' it will so adversely affect the jet's centre of gravity that the pilot will not be able to land back on board the ship.

Below:
Specially built trolleys aid the 'bombheads' in their daily task of shuffling ordnance over a pitching, greasy, deck from the ship's armoury to waiting aircraft. An AIM-9L is comparatively light when compared to a HE bomb, and it takes just two to three sailors to outfit a SHAR with its typical training sortie fit of two acquisition rounds.

No 820 Sqn became the first unit to take the new Sea King HAS 6 on deployment when it embarked on *Ark* for *Westlant 90*, its complement of seven 'cabs' exhibiting a mix of old and new colour schemes for the duration of the cruise. Although this particular helicopter (XV663) is still wearing the midnight blue hue that had been the standard finish for the type since the late 1970s, it has all the added external aerials (particularly the white blade aerial forward of the undercarriage, which is part of the GEC-Marconi AD3400 VHF/UHF secure speech radio fitment) synonymous with the new HAS 6 variant. The FAA has enjoyed good service from its Sea Kings over the past quarter of a century, this particular aircraft having originally entered service in the early 1970s as a HAS 1, before being upgraded to HAS 2A specs later that decade. It was then rebuilt as a HAS 5 (along with thirty-four other HAS 2As) in the early 1980s, prior to finally being upgraded to HAS 6 standard in late 1989. XV663 is seen here preparing to come on board after completing an ASW exercise with one of the task group's escorting frigates.

the latest spec, one had been delivered to the unit fresh from Westland as the first new-build HAS 6, and the final Sea King was still configured as a HAS 5. Commanded by Lt-Cdr N J K Deadman, the unit quickly got to grips with its improved mount, achieving particularly impressive results with the aircraft's new Plessey/GEC Avionics Digital Type 2069 dipping sonar. Although similar to the previous equipment fitted in the HAS 5, the new gear could be dunked to depths of 700ft, rather than just 245ft – all information gleaned by the sonar was now also processed digitally. The deep water of the mid-Atlantic gave the squadron its first chance to test the new rig, and initial reports of its operability were promising.

Following a successful passage across the Atlantic, the *Ark Royal* task force arrived in New York harbour in mid-May, and after a brief period of shore leave, the vessels headed south for the start of a hectic cycle of air ops. For No 820 Sqn this took the form of a LANTSUBASWEX in the Caribbean involving both ships and submarines of the US Sixth Fleet. NAS Mayport, in Florida, then hosted *Ark* for more 'R & R', but while the ship's company enjoyed the leave, No 801 Sqn was hard at work exercising with US Navy A-7Es and F/A-18s during a two-week forward deployment to nearby NAS Cecil Field – Florida Air National Guard F-16As also got in on the act during the det.

With the Sea Harriers back on board by 30 May, *Ark Royal* completed further surface and sub-surface serials, before finally heading eastward for England. After an eventful cruise that had seen the Sea King HAS 6 successfully ushered into fleet service and the Sea Harrier continue to prove itself to be more than a match for the best combat aircraft in service in North America, the *Ark* returned to the North West Wall at Portsmouth naval dockyard on 4 July to bring *Westlant 90* to an end.

XV665 followed a similar career path to its sister-ship featured on page 102, but perhaps looked a little newer on *Westlant 90* thanks to its more up-to-date pale grey paint scheme. In the intervening 25 years since the Sea King was ushered into service with the FAA, the helicopter's external surfaces have become more festooned with aerials, electronic cabling and ESM jammers with each new variant to reach the frontline. Note No 820 Sqn's 'flying fish' emblem aft of the forward crew hatch.

The squadron's sole HAS 5 (XV654) sits shackled to the deck in front of recently-converted HAS 6 XV701 during a 'rotors running' crew change in the mid-Atlantic in May 1990. Both helicopters are being controlled by flightdeck directors, and once the newly strapped-in crews give the signal that they are ready for launch, the FDOs will wave in the deck handlers (drawn from all the various trades working within the unit 'up on the roof') to untether the helicopter, prior to signalling to the pilot that he is cleared to launch. The latter will then wind on seventy per cent of available engine power on the collective pitch and rise into the hover, before carefully pulling away to port and clearing the ship to start the mission, which can last up to three hours.

Prior to the SHARs launching on a typical hour-long sortie, a Sea King AEW 2A will depart and take up station in a pre-arranged operating area some distance away from the carrier. The Thorn EMI ARI 5980/3 Searchwater radar antenna fitted in the inflated 'kettle-drum' radome, and attached to the fuselage via a swivel arm constructed of twelve-inch-diameter steel pipe bought directly from British Gas, works most

effectively at an altitude of 10,000ft – it can track fighter-size targets out to a range of about 125 miles when at this height. A typical crew on board an AEW 2A is made up of a single pilot (who must be a two-tour veteran from either the Sea King ASW or HC 4 communities) and two commissioned observers, each of whom has a display on which to plot targets. The Searchwater radar has been shoehorned in behind the two

displays inside the cabin, and when in operation generates stifling amounts of heat that the purpose-built cooling system has to work hard to keep in check. Flying an AEW 2A is a very demanding job as the helicopter is considerably heavier than the ASW variant, and its surveillance role requires the pilot to single-handedly maintain a smooth and accurate operational profile for hours at a time when on station.

The hardest worked aircraft in the air group during deployment are the Sea King HC 4s, embarked in flight strength to undertake the vertrep mission between the carrier and the various supply ships supporting it. On *Westlant 90* this mission was fulfilled by ZE247 of No 846 Sqn's 'Det 1', the latter usually comprising two to three complete three-man crews (two pilots and an aircrewman) and up to twenty maintenance personnel. A senior lieutenant is usually placed in command of a det of this size.

Embarked Aircraft

No 801 Sqn – Sea Harrier FRS 1
ZD609/000
XZ498/001
ZD582/002
XZ457/003
ZA193/004
ZE693/005
XZ459/006
ZE698/007

No 820 Sqn – Sea King HAS 5/6
XV701/10
ZA129/12

ZG816/13
XV712/14
XV663/15
XV665/17
XV654/18 (HAS 5)

No 846 Sqn 'Det 1' – Sea King HC 4
ZE247/VO

No 849 Sqn 'B' Flight – Sea King AEW 2A
XV672/82
XV649/83
XV704/84

With the flying completed for another day, XV672 of No 849 Sqn's 'B' Flight is struck down to the hangar deck for a spell of sheltered maintenance away from the elements. Note how the impregnated Kevlar fabric that covers the antenna has deflated with the helicopter having been shut down, thus further reducing the amount of space taken up by the machine when not in operation. The two sea-going flights within the FAA's sole AEW unit usually embark three helicopters for a typical deployment.

Ark and the Sea Harrier
FRS 2

Date: November 1990
Location: English Channel
Aircraft Carrier: HMS *Ark Royal* (RO 7)

Today, the Sea Harrier F/A 2 is an integral part of fleet operations from *Invincible* class carriers. The three squadrons equipped with the jet have completed combat tours over Bosnia, patrolled the no-fly zone in northern and southern Iraq and, more recently, carried out exercises with a number of 'out of theatre' nations during the eight-month-long *Ocean Wave 97* deployment to Australasia. Built as a mid-life update for the battle-proven FRS 1, the F/A 2 was designed both structurally (lengthened by fourteen inches) and electronically (Blue Vixen multi-mode radar) around a single weapon – the state-of-the-art Hughes AIM-120 Advanced Medium Range Air-to-Air Missile (AMRAAM). Currently one of the few European combat aircraft using AMRAAM, the F/A 2 is a truly BVR (beyond visual range) capable multi-role fighter.

Although the Sea Harrier F/A 2 is now an extremely effective combat aircraft, back in the summer of 1990 the future of the jet looked far from rosy. The development of the aircraft, and the integration of its systems, had fallen so far behind schedule that the programme was publicly criticised by the House of Commons Defence Committee. The government body claimed that a lack of co-ordination between contractors during the airframe, radar and missile development phases had caused the FRS 2 (as it was then designated) project to be both five years behind schedule and £100 million more expensive than originally budgeted (an increase from £500 to £600 million). The jet's GEC Marconi Avionics Limited Blue Vixen radar was singled out for special criticism, the committee report stating that three years had been lost through technical difficulties associated with the computer software that integrated the system with various other facets of the aircraft. With rumblings concerning the jet's future funding echoing around the corridors at MoD Whitehall and in the Houses of Parliament, both the Navy and British Aerospace pinned their hopes on the Sea Harrier FRS 2 successfully completing its first sea trials in order to keep this crucial programme alive.

HMS *Ark Royal* (RO 7) was chosen as the platform to play host to the first two prototype FRS 2s to operate at sea, and the carrier duly slipped its moorings at Portsmouth's North West Wall early on the morning of 7 November 1990 and sailed into the Channel towards its designated operating area twenty miles south-west of Land's End. Meanwhile, at British Aerospace's small airfield at Dunsfold, in Surrey, Sea Harrier FRS 2s XZ439 and ZA195 were being pre-flighted

British Aerospace Sea Harrier FRS 2 chief project pilot Rod Fredericksen closes on the stern of *Ark Royal* in prototype ZA195 as the carrier sails down the Channel on an unseasonably fine November morning in 1990. Seconds after this photo was taken, the Operation *Corporate* veteran successfully recovered on board the carrier, thus completing the first deck landing made by the new aircraft. Obscured by the Sea Harrier's jet wash is XZ439, the second prototype FRS 2 also embarked for the sea trials. The horseshoe-shaped missile mountings (fitted in place of the Aden cannon pods) for the AIM-120 AMRAAM are clearly visible from this angle.

Fredericksen's gaze is firmly focused on the FDO as he smoothly slides over spot six prior to completing the short flight from Dunsfold airfield in Surrey. The reprofiled nose contours of the F/A 2 have rather spoilt the sleek lines of the second generation SHAR, although I'm sure every Sea Harrier pilot to a man would gladly accept that the reduced aesthetic appeal of his jet is but a small price to pay for the quantum leap in mission capability offered by the Blue Vixen radar, housed within the 'jumboised' radome.

Rod Fredericksen was no stranger to 'blue water' ops, having accumulated over 2,000 hours in the Sea Harrier during his time with the FAA in the 1980s – he has the distinction of being only the second naval pilot to fly an FRS 1, a feat he performed while attached to the A&AEE in 1979. After his stint at Boscombe Down, Lt-Cdr Fredericksen returned to frontline flying with No 800 Sqn, and subsequently saw action over the Falklands in May/June 1982. Mentioned in Dispatches following his destruction of both an Argentine Dagger and a patrol boat, Fredericksen later commanded his wartime unit between May 1985 and February 1988, before resigning his commission and joining British Aerospace as chief project pilot for the FRS 2.

by a joint team of naval and British Aerospace technicians, prior to them being flown out to the carrier. The pilots chosen to perform the first landings were Rod Fredericksen (chief project pilot) and Lt-Cdr Simon Hargreaves (then the FAA's senior pilot at the Aerospace & Armaments Experimental Establishment), both vastly experienced Sea Harrier operators, having flown together in No 800 Sqn during the Falklands War. Two further pilots – Graham Tomlinson (deputy project pilot) and Flt Lt Dave Mackay (A&AEE test pilot) – had embarked on *Ark* at Portsmouth, together with twenty-eight British Aerospace technicians and eight observers from the A&AEE at Boscombe Down in Wiltshire.

The jets duly left their Surrey home with little fuss, and were joined en route to the carrier by two Sea Harrier FRS 1s that had launched from RNAS Yeovilton – the FRS 2's future home. The latter were being flown by the respective COs of Nos 800 and 801 Sqns, Lt-Cdrs R C 'Dick' Hawkins and M W 'Soapy' Watson. The 'four-ship' formation came under the control of the ship's Air Traffic Controllers (call-sign 'Homer') some thirty miles out from landing, and upon overflying *Ark* in the South-west Approaches, the two FRS 2s split off from their escorts and broke into the landing pattern. As chief project pilot, it fell to Rod Fredericksen to complete the first successful shipboard recovery (a Pilot Initiated Approach) in ZA195, and after completing a standard long finals circuit, he selected nozzles down and decelerated into the hover 400 yards aft of the deck. Some 1,000ft behind him, Lt-Cdr Hargreaves repeated the same procedure while keeping a watchful eye on the progress of his formation leader.

The FRS 2 F/A 2 is some 500lb heavier than the FRS 1, but this poses few problems to pilots, who are taught to use ninety-nine per cent of the 104 available for landing in 'dry' conditions. With everything progressing as planned, Fredericksen arrived alongside the number six spot on the deck with his speed matching that of *Ark Royal*. Belying the fact that the jet was in the process of completing its very first carrier landing, the FRS 2 smoothly transitioned across the deck under the scrutiny of the ship's Flightdeck Officer (FDO), as well as countless other pairs of eyes, and once in position, the pilot reduced power momentarily and the jet sank gently down towards the steel 'roof' of *Ark*. Just feet above the deck, Fredericksen pushed open the throttle to help cushion the touchdown, and the aircraft came to rest following a slight power bounce. With his arms outstretched to tell the pilot that he had landed safely, the FDO marshalled the jet forward in order to clear the deck for the recovery of the remaining Sea Harriers.

Within three minutes all four jets had been taken on board safely and were then shackled down and post-flighted. The latter procedure was very much a combined effort shared between the

Not only was XV439 sprayed up in the light grey scheme that would eventually be adopted by all frontline F/A 2s, it was also equipped with an austere version of the Blue Vixen radar in order to check that the system did not interfere with the ship's sensors when in operation. ZA195 was radarless at this stage in the development programme.

While on board, dummy bombs and missiles, plus external tanks, were bolted onto the pylons of both jets to ensure that the aircraft could safely take off and land at differing all-up weights. Both FRS 2s were initially flown on board devoid of external stores (bar the near mandatory 100 Imp gal fuel tanks), the dummy ordnance having been loaded onto the carrier while it was alongside at Portsmouth. Within an hour of ZA195 landing, it had been fitted with twin Sidewinder rails (and dummy AIM-9Ls), as used extensively by the FRS 1 force since 1983. The black and white square marking on the forward fuselage and tail of this jet was applied to facilitate the accurate calibration of photographs taken during weapons release trials.

A British Aerospace engineer readies the hard-tape recording device prior to fitting it into the vacant aft equipment bay of ZA195. This robust piece of equipment was used to record all the control inputs placed on the aircraft's flying surfaces by the pilot while aloft, each reel duly being replaced between sorties. The information encoded on the tape was deciphered below decks using specialised equipment brought on board by the Dunsfold team, who had made one of *Ark Royal*'s squadron ready-rooms their temporary home.

Escorting the two FRS 2s out to *Ark Royal* were a pair of FRS 1s flown by the respective COs of Nos 800 and 801 Sqns, Lt-Cdrs Dick Hawkins and Mike 'Soapy' Watson. The latter is seen here completing his approach to landing in a heavily weathered ZD582, its undersurface smeared with hydraulic fluid and exhaust deposits. This jet was returned to British Aerospace for modification to F/A 2 specification in July 1991, and was subsequently issued to No 899 Sqn in January 1994 following its rework.

ship's aircraft handlers and the civilian engineers embarked for the ten-day trial. While the former topped up the Avtur and replenished the demineralised injection system tank with distillate, the latter would down-load the hard-tape recording device fitted in the aft equipment bay of each FRS 2 and up-load a fresh reel. This piece of kit recorded all the control inputs placed on the aircraft's flying surfaces by the pilot, and once removed, was analysed by technicians below deck through the use of a complex computer system.

During the trial period, which saw some forty-plus sorties generated in variable weather, the jets were launched and recovered in a number of different weapon configurations including dummy AIM-120 AMRAAM rounds, twin AIM-9L Sidewinder rails, and 1,000lb HE bombs. Although both jets looked identical, the two FRS 2s differed internally in the level of equipment fitted: XZ439 boasted an early-build Blue Vixen radar equipped with basic software that allowed limited operability sufficient for deck trials work to be completed, while ZA195 carried no radar at all, having a fully instrumented pitot tube fitted in its place.

The main purpose of the sea trials was to prove the FRS 2's compatibility with the *Invincible* class carriers in respect to the jet's launch and recovery performance, as well as its avionics suitability. When interviewed by the author soon after landing on board *Ark*, Rod Fredericksen described British Aerospace's brief for the aircraft's time at sea as basically a chance to prove that the data gleaned ashore during flight trial from Boscombe Down was indicative of the operational flying environment experienced on board a carrier at sea:

'What we need to show MoD(PE) is that the aircraft is basically an FRS 1 in terms of its deck handling and launch performance, and that the predictions for the FRS 2 configurations work as advertised at sea. I think its launch characteristics are the main crux of the trial, although some avionics data is being accrued along the way.'

Although the sea trials did indeed prove the aircraft's compatibility with its future hosts, ongoing problems with the radar and fire control system continued to slow the programme down, and it wasn't until June 1993 that the Operational Evaluation Unit (OEU), set up to test the jet in frontline conditions, received its first aircraft. In the interim, firing trial had begun with the AIM-120 at Eglin AFB, in Florida, again using XZ439. This facet of the jet's development seemed to go well, and with steady progress being made within the OEU firstly at Boscombe Down, and then at RNAS Yeovilton, the FAA could at last see the day when the redesignated F/A 2 would enter frontline service. The first jet arrived for permanent basing at Yeovilton in September 1993.

Control of the OEU was passed to Sea Harrier training unit No 899 Sqn in mid-1994, and after a series of short embarkations on board carriers in British waters, the squadron finally deployed with four jets to HMS *Invincible* (RO 5) in the Adriatic in September of that same year – fittingly, the det was commanded by squadron boss Lt-Cdr Simon Hargreaves. Operating alongside the FRS 1s of No 800 Sqn, the F/A 2s conducted both CAPs and armed recce sorties over Bosnia during their time on board ship, flying with live ordnance as a standard fitment.

This month-long det paved the way for the first squadron-strength deployment of the F/A 2, which duly occurred on

A solitary No 820 Sqn Sea King was also flown out from its Culdrose home to help share the load of the in demand 'Junglies'. The radar-equipped HAS 6 proved to be particularly useful early on in the trial when it acted as a pathfinder for the radarless HC 4s that had to fly personnel off the ship and back to Cornwall in thick fog.

Opposite:
HC 4 ZD477 dries off in the mid-morning sun after having had a wash down to remove the corrosive sea spray that tends to coat aircraft left chained to the deck for any period of time.

A pair of HC 4 'Junglies' from No 845 Sqn's 'Det 3' were also embarked on *Ark,* being used to ferry personnel to and from RNAS Culdrose, in Cornwall, as well as fulfilling plane guard duties when the FRS 2s were conducting flying ops. A solitary machine from No 707 Sqn was also utilised on the first day of the trials, and it is seen here landing back on board soon after the FRS 2s had recovered after flying in from Dunsfold. The HC 4s frequently served as aerial platforms for the various media, Navy, MoD(PE) and British Aerospace photographers that were embarked to record the trials on film.

26 January 1995 when six aircraft of No 801 Sqn embarked on HMS *Illustrious* (RO 6) in the Channel. After participating in a NATO exercise in the North Atlantic, the carrier headed east for the Adriatic, where it relieved *Invincible* off the coast of Bosnia. Since that first successful deployment, all three frontline Sea Harrier units have re-equipped with the F/A 2, and the true potential of the jet has at last become fully realised in an operational environment.

Embarked Aircraft

A&AEE/British Aerospace –
Sea Harrier FRS 2
XZ439
ZA195

No 820 Sqn – Sea King HAS 6
ZA129/12

No 845 Sqn 'Det 3' – Sea King HC 4
ZA312/B
ZD477/H

No 707 Sqn – Sea King HC 4*
ZD625/ZX

No 800 Sqn – Sea Harrier FRS 1*
XZ495/129

No 801 Sqn – Sea Harrier FRS 1*
ZD582/002

* only stayed on board a single night

Orient Express 92

Date: September 1992
Location: Indian Ocean
Aircraft Carrier: HMS *Invincible* (RO 5)

Up until the late 1960s, Royal Navy carriers were a familiar sight in the warm waters surrounding the former colonies of Singapore, Malaysia and Hong Kong, vessels operating for months at a time with the local navies and air arms of these nations, as well as the Australian and US armed forces. Both the RN and the RAF had important bases on

All is quiet on the rain-sodden deck of HMS *Invincible* as the carrier slowly steams away from Sembawang dock, having spent twelve days alongside at the ex-Royal Navy facility. Only the HC 4s of No 845 Sqn's 'Det 2' and the HAS 5s of No 814 Sqn were on board when this photo was taken, the remaining elements of the air group having had an extended spell ashore at the Royal Singaporean Air Force (RSAF) base at Paya Lebar. Although the Sea King is a large helicopter, various folding mechanisms built into its rotors and tail boom by Sikorsky in response to the US Navy's design brief mean that a series of parked machines can be lashed down close to one another.

Above:
'Junglie' ZD477 is launched for the first flight
of the day in preparation for welcoming back
on board the Sea Harrier FRS 1s of No 800
Sqn and the Sea King AEW 2As of No 849
Sqn 'A' Flight from Paya Lebar. The
aircrewman seated behind the open cabin
door will act as an extra set of eyes for the
pilot during launch and recovery, giving him
information pertaining to the distance he is
away from the deck, and from other
helicopters running-up prior to launch. The
black and grey box bolted to the fuselage
immediately below the red refuelling
receptacle is an antenna for the AN/AAR-47
Missile Approach Warning System (MAWS),
a device which proved essential over Bosnia.

Singapore island at Sembawang, Tengah and Paya Lebar, and they
also utilised the RAAF facility at Butterworth in nearby Malaysia.
Essentially performing a policing role, ensuring that all the newly
independent countries in the region respected one another's
sovereignty, the carrier task group on station in the Far East
personified 'power projection' in its most classical form.

With the creation of defence pacts like SEATO (South-East Asian
Treaty Organisation) and FPDA (Five Power Defence Arrangement),
the stability of the region became more assured as the 1960s
progressed. Concurrently with Asian nations taking more
responsibility for policing the area themselves, the British
government announced swingeing budget cuts which effectively
saw any permanent military presence in the former colonies
removed by 1971, and a number of older carriers like *Victorious*
(R 38) and *Eagle* (R 05) sold off for scrap. RN vessels would continue
to 'show the flag' in the area on a regular basis throughout the
decade, but no carriers ventured this far afield until *Invincible*
undertook her first *Orient Express* in 1983. This deployment was
billed as a showcase for British military technology, and also offered
proof of the RN's ability to mount effective naval operations with
allied navies some considerable distance from home waters. The
cruise lasted over six months, and despite both technical and
political problems plaguing this initial *Orient Express*, others were
performed in 1986 (*Illustrious*) and 1988 (*Ark Royal*), with more
positive results on both fronts.

The intervention of the Gulf War in 1990/1, and the advent of
more pressing commitments to the RN's NATO allies in both the
Mediterranean and Atlantic, saw the next Far East deployment
delayed until 1992, when *Invincible* was again chosen as the
centrepiece for *Orient Express 92*. Embarked on the carrier for its six-
and-a-half-month-long cruise were six Sea Harrier FRS 1s of No 800
Sqn, seven Sea King HAS 5s of No 814 Sqn, two Sea King AEW 2As

Previous page:
The visibility on offer to the pilot in the Sea King is exceptional, as this shot of a HC 4 skirting around the Malaysian island of Pulau Tioman graphically shows. Although the 'Junglie' was performing fine when this photo was taken, the helicopter later suffered a magneto failure while flying over the island, forcing its crew to carry out an emergency autorotation landing at Pulau Tioman airstrip. There it remained for several days before a replacement Rolls-Royce Gnome engine and a team of 'Det 2' technicians were flown in on the second HC 4 to effect repairs.

The first aircraft to return from Paya Lebar were the trio of AEW 2A 'bags' of No 849 Sqn 'A' Flight, which had been acting as fighter directors for both the FAA Sea Harriers and their host's F-16s and F-5Es. The inflated Kevlar 'kettledrum' has been rotated to its stored position prior to the helicopter moving in over the deck for landing. Although flown by a single pilot, the second seat in the AEW 2A is occupied by one of the observers during take-offs and recoveries so as to allow him to take charge of the manual throttle controls in the helicopter in the event of an emergency – a role performed by the co-pilot in an ASW or 'Junglie' 'cab'.

of No 849 Sqn 'A' Flight, and two Sea King HC 4s of No 845 Sqn. In addition to the air group, *Invincible* was joined by the Type 42 destroyer HMS *Glasgow* (D 88), the Type 22 frigate HMS *Boxer* (F 92), and the Type 23 frigate HMS *Norfolk* (F 230). The warships were supported by RFAs *Fort Austin* (A 386) and *Olwen* (A 122).

Having worked-up in the Mediterranean (where a Sea Harrier was lost due to mechanical failure in flight), the vessels proceeded through the Suez Canal and down the East African coast to the US naval base at Diego Garcia – part of the British Indian Ocean Territory, some 1,200 miles north-east of Mauritius. Having replenished its stores, the task group headed north-east towards India for the first of its many exercises with the various armed forces of the region. Port calls in Hong Kong and South Korea followed in the wake of periods of intense operations, before the fleet finally arrived in Singapore for an extended break, prior to participating in the key exercises of the deployment, *Starfish* and *Adex 92-4*.

In order to perform their role in *Starfish*, No 800 Sqn decamped to the Royal Singaporean Air Force (RSAF) base at Paya Lebar, where it operated alongside RSAF F-5Es and F-16As, RAF Tornado F 3s and Harrier GR 7s, RAAF F/A-18As and RNZAF A-4Ks. Previously restricted to surface and sub-surface vessels and ASW assets, *Starfish* saw Sea Harrier FRS 1s provide CAPs alongside Kiwi Skyhawks as they attempted to protect the task group from attacking fast jets launched from other RSAF bases – No 800 Sqn flew between fifteen and twenty sorties a day during the exercise period. Both

types were aided in their tasking by No 849 Sqn's two Sea King AEW 2As, which flew a total of fourteen sorties (accumulating some fifty-five hours on station) during the eight-day exercise. In addition to fulfilling the air intercept role for the defending fighters, the unit also gave warning of incoming raids to the surface vessels involved in *Starfish*.

No 800 Sqn also got to perform the role of attackers during the exercise, flying co-ordinated shipping strikes with the supporting quartet of Flight Refuelling Falcon 20D electronic warfare jets crewed by ex-FAA pilots from the Fleet Requirements and Direction Unit (FRADU) – these had been flown out specially to Singapore from England for *Starfish* and *Adex 92-4*. By the time the exercise was concluded, the Sea Harrier unit had flown some ninety-six sorties in both offensive and defensive roles.

No 814 Sqn had also been kept busy during the ASW phase of *Starfish*, deploying two 'cabs' to RFA *Fort Austin* for the duration of the exercise. The primary target for the 'pingers' was the RAN Oberon class submarine HMAS *Ovens* (S 70), which proved to be a worthy adversary in the warm and shallow waters off Singapore island – geographical features that have traditionally helped the submariner avoid detection by sonar or radar.

After another spell alongside at Sembawang, *Invincible* sailed back into the congested waters surrounding Singapore and welcomed No 800 Sqn back on board, before heading north up the east coast of Malaysia in preparation for *Adex 92-4*. Unlike *Starfish*,

An 'Aardvark' observer strides back across the deck in the direction of the island, having vacated his recently returned AEW 2A. While he is debriefed back in the flight's ready-room, his helicopter will be struck down to the hangar bay for a period of post-detachment maintenance, thus assuring its operability for the up-and-coming *Adex 92-4* exercise.

Trailing in the wake of the Sea King 'bags' (as the fast jet pilots call them) were five SHARs of No 800 Sqn, all of which used the added boost of water injection to ensure that they had adequate power on hand to land back safely aboard ship. The addition of pressurised water (the centrally-mounted tank within the jet holds 30-Imp gal, which can be exhausted in just ninety seconds) into the Pegasus engine's combustion chamber raises its thrust level from 104 (dry) to 108 per cent – essentially an extra 1,000lb of thrust – through cooling the turbine and thus allowing it to spin faster without the risk of overheating, although the latter figure is degraded because of the 'hot and humid' conditions encountered in the Far East. Steam and droplets of water can be seen venting from the overflow tubes positioned just ahead of the forward nozzles on XZ459 as the jet approaches the carrier. The use of water also reduces the critical nozzle JPT (Jet Pipe Temperature), meaning that the count rate on the engine life recorder is also lowered – the JPT figure is usually 50°F higher (700°F compared with 650°F) in the Far East than it is back in the UK. Note that this aircraft lacks the twin Aden pods fitted beneath its fuselage centre section, the squadron choosing to delete the option of cannon armament for much of the deployment in order to reduce the jet's all-up weight while operating in the energy-sapping climate.

Opposite:
A six-month-long deployment away from RNAS Yeovilton places a severe strain on the engineering department within a SHAR unit, and this was further increased for No 800 Sqn in 1992 because only six FRS 1s were available to take on *Orient* due to the FRS 2 return to works programme then having priority over airframes. That said, the half dozen jets embarked proved to be thoroughly reliable throughout the trip, although a single FRS 1 (ZA193) was lost in a non-fatal accident soon after the carrier had deployed. Just how intense the flying programme undertaken by the unit was during the *Starfish/Adex 92-4* period was can be gauged by the badly chipped intake lip and wing leading edges on this jet. Both areas were soon retouched after the exercises had been completed.

Safely back on board, and with the engine shut down, FRS 1 ZE691 is set upon by the deck handlers of No 800 Sqn, who immediately insert the red-tagged safety locks and charge pins in the outriggers and external stores pylons – the pilot will have repeated the same procedure inside the cockpit with his Martin-Baker ejection seat. Meanwhile 'up front' the tow tractor is positioned to push the jet back aft, where the engineering personnel will fill the tanks with 8,000lb of Avtur, top up the water injection reservoir, and check the engine oil and hydraulics levels. This all takes about forty-five minutes, after which the aircraft will be declared available for its next sortie. Rebuilt as a F/A 2, ZE691 is currently serving with No 899 Sqn.

the latter exercise focused exclusively on air defence, and had been structured specially to test the region's Integrated Air Defence System (IADS), as set up by the signatories (Malaysia, Singapore, Britain, Australia and New Zealand) of the FPDA some years earlier, and the effective integration of *Invincible*'s task group into this system. No fewer than 120 aircraft were committed to the exercise, which took place over a three-day period off the coast of the Malaysian island of Pulau Tioman.

Again, No 800 Sqn was in the thick of things, flying both attack and defensive sorties with the help of No 849 Sqn AEW 2As and RSAF E-2s. In order to increase the effectiveness of the latter asset, two Singaporean fighter controllers were embarked on *Invincible* for the duration of *Adex 92-4*. As part of their fleet defence role, the Sea Harrier unit operated a 'flexi-deck' policy (as opposed to its more routine 'two over two'), whereby two jets would launch just prior to a pair of FRS 1s recovering after an hour-long CAP. To further increase the jet's time on station, full use was made of the available air refuelling assets, which took the form of several VC10K 2 tankers that had deployed to Kuala Lumpur International Airport as part of the large RAF contingent sent out for the exercise from Britain and Germany. As an example of the sortie times that could be achieved with a Sea Harrier FRS 1 toting a bolt-on refuelling probe, the unit's CO, Lt-Cdr D D 'Dave' Braithwaite (a Falklands War veteran with No 801 Sqn), flew for almost five hours non-stop on a CAP thanks to regular top-ups of Avtur. A variety of targets was encountered by the FRS 1 pilots during their patrols, ranging from RSAF F-16s to Malaysian A-4s and MB-339As.

Having completed the two main exercises of the deployment by the end of September, the task group returned to Hong Kong for a final port call in the Far East, before heading westwards across the Indian Ocean and back through the Suez Canal into the more familiar waters of the eastern Mediterranean. Apart from a brief spell operating over Cypriot bombing ranges while shore-based at

Below:
Unlike most frontline fast jets, the Sea Harrier (in both FRS 1 and F/A2 guises) relies on a drag-inducing bolt-on refuelling probe rather than a built-in device. The latter fixture is becoming more commonplace in the SHAR world, rather than being seen as an optional extra only dusted off for long-range ferry trips. This is primarily because frontline units are being tasked with operating further afield from the carrier, as turned out to be the case over Bosnia-Herzegovina. With the fuel-critical Sea Harrier, a typical sortie will see the jet launch with 8,000lb of Avtur on board, which will allow the pilot to fly a forty-five-to sixty-minute mission, depending on the specifics of the flight involved – heavy ACM means greater fuel usage than on a high level armed recce or CAP. By using the refuelling probe, the jet can top off its tanks prior to transiting to its patrol area, or alternatively replenish its stock of Avtur on the return leg to the carrier. ZE693 is sat idling on the stern of the carrier while waiting its turn to launch.

Akrotiri in early November, the air wing kept itself busy performing a routine programme with other task group assets. Finally, on the 26th of the month the embarked aircraft flew off the carrier for Culdrose (Nos 814 and 849 Sqns) and Yeovilton (Nos 800 and 845 Sqns) as *Invincible* sailed back into the Channel after almost seven months away.

As this book went to press, the latest Far East deployment – *Ocean Wave 97* – was underway, marking the first time a RN task group has ventured into the Indian Ocean since *Orient Express 92*.

Embarked Aircraft

No 800 Sqn – Sea Harrier FRS 1
ZD580/122
ZD611/123
ZE691/124
XZ459/125
ZA193/126*
ZD579/126
ZE693/127

* crashed off Cyprus on 28 May 1992

No 814 Sqn – Sea King HAS 5

ZD630/65
ZA169/66
ZD633/67
ZD637/68
ZE419/69
XV710/70
ZG818/71

No 845 Sqn 'Det 2' – Sea King HC 4
ZD477/A
ZA312/B

No 849 Sqn 'A' Flight – Sea King AEW 2A
XV664/185
XV650/186
XV656/187

Left:
No 800 Sqn deployed with nine pilots from Yeovilton for the *Orient 92* cruise, seven of which were in the process of completing their first frontline tours. Only the unit's CO, Lt-Cdr 'Dave' Braithwaite, had experienced an extended deployment before (*Orient Express 83*), while his Senior Pilot, Lt-Cdr Dave Baddams, had previously seen service in the Far East from the deck of HMAS *Melbourne* (A 21) in an A-4G Skyhawk. Lt Paul Stone was one of the 'first timers', and he has since gone on to complete a tour with No 899 Sqn as an instructor, which included deploying to *Invincible* in an F/A 2 in September 1994 as part of the latter jet's first exposure to frontline flying over Bosnia-Herzegovina.

FOD (Foreign Object Debris) guards are fitted as soon as the engine has shut down, these devices protecting the compressor blades from the detritus that can be blown around on the exposed deck of an aircraft carrier when underway. They are removed from the jet just prior to engine ignition and stored securely behind the island.

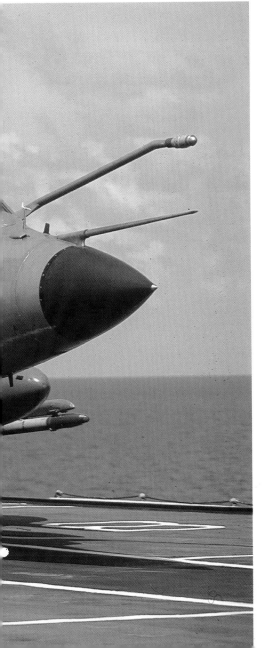

With his green launch flag raised aloft and rippling in the wind, the FDO sends the SHAR on its way from his position behind the white wingtip safety line. The acceleration of the Sea Harrier is breathtaking, the jet racing from zero to ninety knots in just a matter of feet after the pilot has gone 'brakes off' once the power output of the Pegasus has reached fifty-five per cent.

Opposite:
'SPLOT' Dave Baddams hands ZD580's logbook down to a waiting technician, who will return it to the squadron's maintenance office in the hangar deck. Any technical snag encountered while strapped into the SHAR is noted in this volume upon the pilot's return, accompanied by his signature. Once the problem has been rectified, the engineer who has either carried out the repair, or checked that it has been completed correctly, will also sign his name alongside the relevant work order so as to ensure that the aircraft's

maintenance history is complete in every detail. As mentioned earlier, 'Aussie' Baddams had flown Skyhawks with the RAN in the early 1980s before joining the FAA after his beloved A-4Gs had been sold to New Zealand – three of the A-4Ks he flew against during *Adex 92-4* featured in his logbook! He assumed the position of 'SPLOT' from Operation *Corporate* veteran Lt-Cdr Simon Hargreaves in early September 1992, bringing to the squadron his vast wealth of experience accrued during 3,000-plus hours of fast jet flying.

Left:
Invincible's island structure juts out from behind the massive Type 909 antenna dome which guides the vessel's primary defensive weapon, the Sea Dart missile – the remaining domes house SCOT secured communications antennae. Immediately above the radar is the bridge, or Compass Platform in true navy parlance. The flat dish-like structure bolted onto the roof of the bridge is a satellite communications receiver, and the lattice-style revolving antenna is an integral part of the Type 1022 long-range air warning radar suite.

Opposite:
One of the many helicopters that 'cross-decked' with *Invincible* during the exercise period was a diminutive Westland Wasp HAS 1 of the RNZAF's No 3 Sqn, which was embarked on the fleet oiler HMNZS *Endeavour* (A 11) – hence the Dayglo orange 'ER' in 'OILER' on the aircraft's nose. The air force operates seven Wasps on behalf of the navy, these helicopters usually going to sea on board the latter's modest fleet of *Leander*-class frigates.

Operation *Grapple*

Date: March 1993
Location: Adriatic Sea
Aircraft Carrier: HMS *Ark Royal* (RO 7)

Emphasising the nature of No 801 Sqn's recent deployment to the instrumented NATO range at Deci, on the island of Sardinia, two Sea Harriers return to the carrier equipped with three Carrier Bomb/Light Stores (CBLSs) apiece. The APC undertaken by the unit over a two-week period in March 1993 was a first for the FRS 1, and was performed because of the restrictions placed on the squadron by Italian authorities with respect to low-flying operations over Italy. When compared with the type of missions flown against the ranges in the UK by the FRS 1 community, the det proved to be of limited value due to restrictions on routeing into the target area itself.

As the break-up of the former Yugoslavia spiralled into open civil war in 1991/2, and the situation in the newly-created Republic of Bosnia-Herzegovina worsened with Bosnian Serb factions fighting Bosnian Muslims for control of the country, firstly the UN, then NATO and the WEU (Western Economic Union), stepped in to try to broker a peace deal between the warring factions. Reports of atrocities on the ground eventually led to the UN sending in troops in an effort to create 'safe havens' for civilian victims of the fighting, while an arms blockade was simultaneously set up both on land and at sea by NATO forces. As early as August 1992 the UN ordered the airspace over Bosnia-Herzegovina closed to military aircraft, but continual violations by both the Serbs and the Muslims eventually saw Operation *Deny Flight* instigated in April 1993, involving literally hundreds of NATO aircraft mounting standing patrols over the battle-scarred region.

As part of the force build-up in support of the UN effort, the RN deployed a six-ship task group to the Adriatic with the carrier *Ark Royal* as its centrepiece; Secretary of State for Defence Malcolm Rifkind announced in Parliament on 14 January 1993 that the additional vessels were being deployed in an effort to deter further attacks on British forces. Although not strictly part of any recognised NATO or WEU operation, *Ark* and her escorts – Type 22 frigates HMS *Broadsword* (F 88) (later replaced by sister-ship *Brilliant* (F 90)), which was in turn relieved by the Dutch *Kortenaer* class frigate HMNLS *Abraham Crijnssen* (F 816) and *Coventry* (F 98), plus the RFA's *Fort Grange* (A 385) and *Olwen* (A 122) – took up station off the Bosnian coast in late January, and proceeded to operate within the cramped environs of the Adriatic until July. Embarked on the carrier at the start of its lengthy deployment were eight Sea Harrier FRS 1s of No 801 Sqn, three Sea King AEW 2As of No 849 Sqn's 'B' Flight, and eight Sea King HC 4s of No 846 Sqn – six Royal Artillery 105mm howitzers and assorted Commando, Royal Marine and Army airborne troops also formed an integral part of the task group.

Prior to sailing into the Mediterranean, the carrier completed an intensive work-up phase off Gibraltar which saw the HC 4s undertaking troop drills at Lathbury Barracks with 94 Locating Regiment Royal Artillery, as well as further exercises with other ground force elements at the Windmill Hill ranges on the British dependency. An *Adex* was also hastily arranged for the benefit of the SHARs and Sea King AEWs, involving Gibraltar-based RAF Tornados, Hawks and Buccaneers, plus FRADU Hunters, Falcons and Canberras. Once in the Adriatic, the presence of the carrier group seemed to deter the Serbian and Muslim armies from

Opposite:
Operation *Grapple* was dominated by the Sea King HC 4, with both Nos 845 and 846 Sqns embarking in full strength so as to be able to fulfil all possible mission taskings in support of British forces on the ground in Bosnia. This effectively meant that for the first eight weeks of 1993 sixteen 'Junglies' were on station either ashore at the Forward Operating Base at Split, in Croatia, or at sea on board the 'LPH' *Ark Royal*. Here, 'Victor Mike' (ZD478) prepares for the short return flight to the airhead at Bari airport during a vertrep off the Italian coast – note the load-carrying hoist lying on the flightdeck beneath the helicopter.

In addition to dropping ordnance on parched Sardinian soil, No 801 Sqn's pilots indulged in more typical Dissimilar Air Combat Training (DACT) when back on board *Ark Royal*. Due to the cramped confines of the Adriatic Sea, and the close proximity of the French carrier *Clemenceau* (R 98) and the American 'supercarrier' USS *John F Kennedy* (CV 67), finding allied aircraft 'game for a tussle' was never a problem. During the first four months of the deployment the SHARs duelled firstly with French Super Etendards and Crusaders, followed by F-14s and F/A-18s from 'Big John'. Some cross-decking of pilots also took place in order to better cement the rules of engagement between the various navies. Stained and smeared in the wake of nineteen days of near constant flying from Deci, ZD607 returns to *Ark* for a period of post-det maintenance. The full-colour chequered rudder markings synonymous with No 801 Sqn in the early to mid-1980s were reapplied with the approval of squadron boss Lt-Cdr Tim Mannion, soon after he assumed command of the unit from 'Soapy' Watson in November 1992.

attacking the British forces on the ground, at least in the short term. In order to keep themselves active while standing at readiness off shore, the RN vessels participated in a series of exercises with firstly the French National Task Group, led by the carrier *Clemenceau* (R 98), and then the US Sixth Fleet's USS *Theodore Roosevelt* (CVN 71) Battle Group. The Italian Navy also invited *Ark* to exercise with it in the Ionian Sea.

Two months prior to the carrier group arriving, RFA Argus (A 135) had deployed to the region with four Sea King HC 4s of No 845 Sqn's 'B' Flight (later redesignated 'Det 4') as part of Operation *Grapple*. These aircraft, plus the associated Commando Helicopter Operations and Support Cell (CHOSC), were pressed into service with the British element of the UN Protection Force (UNPROFOR) in

SHARs litter the deck following the mass
return of the unit from Sardinia on the
morning of 31 March 1993. These jets were
either pushed aft or struck down to the
hangar deck for essential maintenance.

Bosnia-Herzegovina. Indeed, over the next three-and-a-half years the HC 4 'Junglies' of the FAA would see more active service in the region than any other British aircraft type.

Returning to 1993, once it was realised that the carrier task group was not going to have to instigate any immediate evacuation of British troops from the region, four of No 846 Sqn's HC 4s were returned to Yeovilton in mid-March in order to allow routine low-level night vision goggles (NVG) training to continue – proficiency in this crucial area had been drastically affected when two thirds of the frontline force had been hastily despatched to the Adriatic. The remaining helicopters continued to fly in theatre under the guise of 'Det 4', crews operating on a rotational basis from Yeovilton in order to keep proficient in low-level flying. In order to try to save the time and effort (not to mention the cost) expended in continually flying crews to and from the Adriatic, the RN asked their Italian counterparts if NVG training could be performed over Italy, but permission was not forthcoming. Two Sea Harriers also returned to Yeovilton when it was realised that there was no need for an enhanced unit strength. The quartet of HC 4s was kept busy in the vertrep (vertical replenishment) role, shuttling supplies and personnel between the RN's airheads and the fleet offshore. When flying at night or in poor weather, the crews would use NVGs to complete their tasks safely. A Global Positioning System and an AN/AAR-47 Missile Approach Warning System (MAWS) were also fitted to each HC 4, and these proved invaluable throughout the deployment.

While No 846 Sqn shuttled between ship and shore, No 849 Sqn's 'B' Flight was kept busy operating with aircraft from the

Three of the four HC 4s that remained on board *Ark Royal* to form 'Det 4' following the return of half of No 846 Sqn to Yeovilton in mid-March 1993 are seen idling on the deck of the carrier between shuttle missions. Unlike No 845 Sqn's frontline 'cabs', which donned an all-white United Nations-inspired paint scheme and received added protective 'goodies' like armoured crew seats, Kevlar floor armour, MAWS, upgraded floodlighting, improved 'Have Quick' multi-frequency radios and Mode 4 IFF, the carrier-based helicopters were retained pretty much in stock condition.

French and US navies, as well their own FAA assets. In addition to their more conventional AEW role, crews functioned as makeshift Air Traffic Controllers and used their Searchwater radar to keep a watchful eye on vessels operating within Bosnian and Croatian coastal waters.

The lull in the fighting in March also allowed No 801 Sqn to send five of its six FRS 1s, nine pilots and 110 maintainers to the sophisticated weapons range at Decimomannu, on the Italian island of Sardinia, for three weeks of solid ground attack exercising. Bearing in mind the future role of the Sea Harrier in NATO's 'shooting' war over Bosnia in 1994/5, this training proved to be rather fortuitous, despite the unit not firing a shot in anger on this particular deployment. Although Sea Harrier squadrons had regularly visited Deci's Air Combat Manoeuvring Instrumentation (ACMI) range over the years, no FAA unit had ever performed an APC (Armament Practice Camp) before. Charting new ground, No 801 Sqn (led by Lt-Cdr T S 'Tim' Mannion) performed 140-plus close air support sorties utilising dedicated forward air controllers. Conventional and loft bombing attacks with live ordnance, rocket strafing, and precision photo-recce of heavily defended targets comprised the bulk of the missions flown. Prior to the Deci sojourn, the unit had been working on its practice intercepts (PIs) both within the squadron itself and against French, Italian and US Navy aircraft.

Complementing the pilots' increased effectiveness in their secondary air-to-ground role, their FRS 1s had also had their defensive weapons suite improved through the fitment of AN/ALE-40 chaff/flare dispensers and Mode 4 IFF equipment, the latter making the Sea Harriers compatible with other NATO air assets in the region. A further mod hastily fitted to the jet prior to departure –

Clear of RFA *Olwen*'s stern helicopter deck, ZG819 slowly climbs away from the fleet oiler on yet another 'grocery run' back to *Fort Grange*. No 820 Sqn dubbed *Grapple* 'Yugotours 93', stating that the only thing they dropped in anger during the deployment was 'the odd courgette or carton of milk'! Joking aside, the unit gained valuable experience in operating two to four helicopters simultaneously from single spot ships.

and greatly welcomed by the pilots – was a commercially available GPSs, Velcroed to the cockpit instrument coaming!

The extra Sea Harriers and Sea King HC 4s embarked on _Ark_ at the start of the deployment meant that No 820 Sqn had had to operate its six HAS 6s from _Fort Grange_ (four 'cabs') and _Olwen_ (two) throughout this initial patrol. With no realistic sub-surface threat on offer in the cramped and shallow confines of the Adriatic, the unit struggled to find an ASW role to perform. Indeed, it was only when the task group moved into the Ionian Sea for an exercise with other RN vessels (including submarines) that the squadron got to reacquaint itself with its primary tasking. In addition to helping supplant the HC 4s in vertrep operations, No 820 Sqn completed a number of surface search (SURSEARCH) missions in an effort to stop blockade runners entering Croatian or Bosnian ports.

Ark Royal was relieved in the Mediterranean by _Invincible_ in July 1993, thus starting a routine of Adriatic patrols that would last until early 1996. Although this initial deployment had been hurriedly despatched to counter a hostile threat, no shots were fired by the FAA in anger throughout the task group's six months on station. Sadly, this did not remain the case for future deployments.

Opposite:
With the surface and sub-surface threat to the task group perceived to be low in the Adriatic, _Ark Royal_'s ASW assets in the form of No 820 Sqn were deployed on board RFAs' _Fort Grange_ (four 'cabs') and _Olwen_ (two – this detachment was designated No 820A Flt) for the duration of _Grapple_. Apart from performing periodic CASEXs and SURFEXs in the less restricted waters of the Ionian Sea, the principal tasking of the unit in theatre was the delivery of groceries to various ships in the task group. New-build Sea King HAS 6 ZG819 (nicknamed '_ARRY_) hailed from No 820A Flt, as denoted by the small nose art on the battery compartment door situated between the Racal MIR-2 'Orange Crop' ESM antennae.

Embarked Aircraft

No 801 Sqn – Sea Harrier FRS 1
ZD581/000
ZD607/001
XZ492/002
ZE694/003
ZD614/004
XZ459/005*
ZD691/006**
ZE693/007*
ZE692/713***

* returned to RNAS Yeovilton by 1/3/93
** returned to RNAS Yeovilton 18/1/93
*** ex-No 899 Sqn jet sent to replace '006'

No 846 Sqn – Sea King HC 4
ZE428/VH*
ZA299/VJ*
ZF117/VK
ZE426/VL
ZD478/VM
ZA291/VN*
ZA293/VO*
ZD480/VP**

* returned to RNAS Yeovilton by 1/3/93
** formerly 'C' with No 845 Sqn

No 849 Sqn 'B' Flight – Sea King AEW 2A
XV650/182
XV672/183
XV649/184